Flight of the Garuda
The Dzogchen Songs of Shabkarpa

A Modern Translation
by Dr. Nida Chenagtsang

SKY
PRESS

Back cover image by Liz Sung.

Published by:

Sky Press

Pure Land Farms
3265 Santa Maria Road
Topanga, CA 90290

www.skypresspublications.com

Copyright © 2026 by Nida Chenagtsang
རྒྱལ་སྲིད་ཡོད་ཀྱི་གསོ་རིག་ཁང་།

All rights reserved.

No part of this book may be reproduced in any form or by any means,
electronic or mechanical, including photocopying, recording,
or by any information storage and retrieval system, without
permission in writing from the publisher.

ISBN: 9781950153343

Editor: Tenzin Wainwright
Design and Typesetting: Pearse Gaffney
First English Edition
Printed on acid-free paper

Special thanks to all whose valuable contributions
made this work possible.

ཆོས་རྒྱལ་དངག་དབང་དར་རྒྱས།

Chogyal Ngawang Dargye (1740-1807 CE)

ཞབས་དཀར་ཚོགས་དྲུག་རང་གྲོལ་

Shabkar Tsokdruk Rangdrol (1781 to 1851 CE)

མཁའ་ལྡིང་གཤོག་རྒྱབས་
Flight of the Garuda

ཞབས་དཀར་ཚོགས་དྲུག་རང་གྲོལ་
Shabkar Tsokdruk Rangdrol

Contents

Publisher's Note x

Introduction by Dr. Nida xiii

Introduction by Shabkarpa 3

Song 1   What a Surprise! 07
Song 2   Mind is the Essence of All Teachings 11
Song 3   Cut the Root 17
Song 4   Introduction to the Ground of Mind 26
Song 5   Introduction to the Ground of Delusion 30
Song 6   Pointing out the Nature of Mind 36
Song 7   You Know 42
Song 8   Look Directly at Your Own Mind 53
Song 9   Magic Projection 64
Song 10 All in the Mind 70
Song 11 Emptiness, Appearance, Awareness 89
Song 12 Recognizing the Ground's Three Kayas 95
Song 13 Self Liberation of Five Toxins 102
Song 14 Self Liberation of Six Sensorial Experiences 114
Song 15 Stillness, Motion, Awareness 122
Song 16 One Taste 127
Song 17 View, Meditation, Lifestyle, & Result 137
Song 18 Beyond Meditation 152
Song 19 Present Awareness 165
Song 20 Mastery of Nonduality 175
Song 21 Overcoming Obstacles 179
Song 22 The Five Buddhas are Within 195
Song 23 Life is the Teaching 199

About Dr. Nida Chenagtsang 210

Publisher's Note:

In 2016, I had the great privilege of traveling to Amdo, Tibet with Dr. Nida Chenagtsang and a group of Tibetan medicine students to study Sowa Rigpa and experience local nomad culture. After the group left, I stayed on to do a personal retreat in the ngakpa village of Rigzin Rabpel Ling in the Rebkong area where Dr. Nida is closely spiritually connected. After my retreat concluded, Dr. Nida came to visit the yogis and yoginis of the village and through the coming together of auspicious circumstances, it was arranged for him to offer a teaching on the topic of the *Flight of the Garuda* to the local practitioners in the beautiful village temple.

This teaching is particularly beloved by the meditators of the region, since Shabkarpa was a famous Amdo yogi who spent years in solitude in a cave very close by, which our group also had the opportunity to visit. I was the only foreigner in attendance at this special teaching, and Dr. Nida taught in his native Amdo language without translation. Yet the transmission of the teaching was palpable, beyond words, and the unwavering attention of the audience of Rebkong yogis and yoginis is something that I will not forget.

During the breaks, Dr. Nida would share some explanations with me, especially pointing out the modern metaphors that he used to help the practitioners connect more personally and authentically with the instruction. I hold this memory very close to my heart, and the *Flight of the Garuda* is a text that I have continued to read and contemplate over the last decade.

I'm so happy to see Dr. Nida's new translation of *Flight of the Garuda* come into print and be made available for a wider audience. His mastery of the English language and modern choice of words combined with his close connection to both the spiritual lineage

and geographic home of Shabkar makes this work truly special. I'd like to sincerely thank Tenzin Wainwright for his hard work and meticulousness in compiling this text, working very closely with Dr. Nida to clarify all questions.

We have included the original Tibetan verses for students of Tibetan language, as well as the phonetics, to encourage practitioners to sing these dharma songs, in the way that yogis and yoginis of the past would sing, high up on the vast Tibetan plateau, using their voices to support the recognition of the essence of mind. May these songs continue to be sung — in Tibetan, in English, in your own language, and in your own words and melodies, so that they will speak to your own heart and mind! Like all authentic dharma teachings, these verses carry their deepest benefit when received in the traditional way, through direct oral transmission and instruction from teacher to student.

Christiana Polites
January 2026 at Pure Land Farms California

www.skypresspublications.com | sowarigpainstitute.org

Introduction by Dr. Nida

The *Flight of Garuda* is an amazing meditation text, originally known as the *Dzogchen Tawé Luyang Kading Shoklap*. *Dzogchen* རྫོགས་ཆེན་ (short for *Dzogpa Chenpo*) is commonly translated as the 'Great Perfection' or the 'Great Completion,' but I like to use Professor Robert Thurman's translation, the 'Great Connection,' from the Sanskrit term, mahasandhi. *Tawa* ལྟ་བའི་ means the 'View,' and *Luyang* གླུ་དབྱངས་ means the 'Song,' so the full title is "The Song of the View of Great Connection and the Power of the Garuda's Flight".

It was written by Shabkar Tsokdruk Rangdrol, who is one of the most famous Tibetan historical meditators and wandering yogis. Shabkarpa was a traveler, a writer, a singer, and overall a very famous meditator. Even from his birth he had innate spiritual qualities and visionary experiences. He grew up in the farming region of Rebkong, northeastern Tibet. His family were farmers, so as a young boy, he was helping his mother and sister to try to improve their quality of life. But he was very interested in the Dharma, and he studied how to read and write, and very quickly he perfected his basic studies. He started joining the local Ngakpa community for pujas and rituals. He was very good at memorizing and chanting, so also individually he started performing rituals too. Then he received some offerings and donations, and he used those donations to help the local community and his family.

When he heard the name of his root teacher, Chogyal Ngawang Dargye, he felt an instant connection without any doubt and decided to go to meet him. His teacher was actually the local Mongolian

Shukseb Jetsun Choying Zangmo

With my teacher the Yogini Ani Ngawang Gyaltsen

king, the regent of my hometown (Malho-Sogdzon), in the Qinghai province, Huangnan Prefecture. Malho རྨ་ལྷོ་ means 'South Yellow River', a kind of district. Our place is called the Mongolian county of Malho. At that time, it was considered a Mongolian land, but the culture was a Tibetan and Mongolian blend, completely integrated like a melting pot. We speak the Tibetan language and dress like Tibetans, but we live in Mongolian yurts with livestock—yaks, sheep, horses, goats, mastiffs— like nomadic people. We had our own local king and that king, Chogyal (meaning Dharma King), Ngawang Dargye, was not only the king; he was also a great spiritual master, spreading teachings and giving empowerments.

When Shabkarpa went to see him, he accepted Shabkarpa very well, because, even though he was a royal king, the teacher reconized that Shabkarpa would be a great practitioner. Shabkarpa was first trained in the very basic preliminary practices and he was trained in *Lam Rim* which is 'The Stages of the Path' in the Gelugpa system of study. He studied in a very sutric way, read all the texts, and received teachings from his master, asking questions. So back and forth, he studied completely, and then he did the Nyingma Ngöndro practices and received many teachings and empowerments. They became very close as disciple and a master. Their story is a little bit similar to Marpa and Milarepa.

The Dharma King suggested that Shabkarpa do a three-year retreat, which he did at a place called Tayanchi ཟླ་ཡན་ཆི་ which means "the cave of the yogis" and is also in my hometown. Shabkarpa spent three years meditating there and built a very strong base of meditation, having lots of experiences and meditative visions. Throughout his whole lifetime, Shabkarpa received teachings and instructions, and remained very humble, a really great master. He would go to meet many teachers from all different schools to receive teachings, to improve his knowledge, and many of them in return asked him to give them teachings and transmissions.

The Flight of Garuda

Shabkar's Cave in Amdo, Tibet

✢ Introduction by Dr. Nida

Shabkarpa continued his journey from cave to cave, mountain to mountain, land to land, walking the Tibet high plateau by foot as a wandering yogi. In every place he spent a lot of time meditating, giving teachings and writing songs. He was constantly engaged in dharma activities but meanwhile he also was very kind and very humble, giving to others and supporting people he met on his path. Sometimes he received offerings of food or livestock, and then if he met anybody poor, who was in need, he would without any doubt give the gifts to them. So Shabkarpa was very generous and very kind. When he travelled to central Tibet, he also became a vegetarian, and he became one of the most famous vegetarian masters in the history of Tibetan Buddhism.

In the year 1806, Shabkar entered a rigorous three-year retreat at Tso Nying མཚོ་སྙིང་ ("The Heart of the Lake"), an island in the vast, Turquoise Kokonor Lake. Access to the island was not possible by boat; instead, it could only be reached by foot when the ice covered the lake for a brief period each year. Yogins would bring a year's worth of supplies and seek perfect solitude on this island. During this retreat, Shabkar mostly practiced the Tamdrin-Pagmo (Hayagriva and Vajravarahi) cycle of teachings, but it was also during this deep immersion that he composed the *Flight of Garuda*.

The *Flight of Garuda* is considered the essence of his teachings, all his life experience, and his spiritual understanding. It synthesizes various approaches, including elements such as analytic meditation and Vipassana alongside aspects of Mahamudra and, of course, the Dzogchen *Trekchö* views. Trekchö ཁྲེགས་ཆོད་ means 'Cutting Through Hardness', or we can call it the "Loosen-up Path" so that's why he really focuses on the view. We can understand the *Flight of Garuda* according to any Dharma tradition or meditation text. Whether you practice Zen, Shamatha, Vipassana, Ati-yoga, Madhyamika, Mahamudra, or even if you are more interested in performing rituals, this book is really important, because it really shows the essence in a very bold, very simple, direct way.

Shabkarpa's writings are distinct from those of many scholars who share information in a very intellectual and academic style. Although he was also very well-versed in numerous texts, teachings, and commentaries, he wrote everything from his own personal experience. That's why we call it *Drup Thup Gi Lu*, གྲུབ་ཐོབ་ཀྱི་གླུ་ experienced yogi style. This experiential approach makes his teachings exceptionally clear, direct, and accessible for everyone. Actually his style is very similar to that of Yuthok — free flow, very bold, and very direct. He doesn't aim to prove his point or assert his correctness; instead, he gently and kindly shares his understanding of what *Dzogpa Chenpo* is. I don't need to say many things; people should read the book—the teachings speak for themselves.

I have a very special personal connection with this *Flight of the Garuda*. Shabkar passed the teachings down to his heart disciple, Pema Gyatso, who was teaching mostly in central Tibet. Pema Gyatso's heart disciple is Ani Lochen from Shukseb nunnery, who was considered one of the greatest Tibetan yoginis of the 20th century. Of course she received many teachings from many masters, but her main Dzogpa Chenpo practice was this *Flight of Garuda* which she received directly from Pema Gyatso and then became the lineage holder. Ani Lochen also had many disciples and was teaching the nuns and monks and yogis and yoginis. She gave this teaching to my teacher, Ani Ngawang Gyaltsen. When I received this teaching from Ani-la in my early twenties, it was a one-to-one teaching in Lhasa. She gave me the teaching and basic instructions, and then asked me to meditate. So, receiving the transmission, meditating, and then asking questions—I tried to enhance my practice. So this lineage — Shabkarpa, Pema Gyatso, Ani Lochen, and Ani Ngawang—between Shabkarpa and me, there are three great masters, which I feel is very fortunate.

I have kept this as my practice for many years, and I consider it like my jewel. I considered for a long time if I should teach this publicly or not — maybe I was a little bit stingy about sharing this publicly, I had a personal attachment about this. But we are ageing, our ideas change, and we become more generous. And since I have been teaching different meditations and techniques, I thought now is a good time to also teach this *Flight of the Garuda*. There are already translations published, and of course, other masters are teaching this too. But from my side, I just open myself, open my mind, and now I want to share this with a good intention to really help people.

Today there is so much spiritual confusion. So many people are really spiritually confused because there are so many schools, so many different styles of teachings, and so many ways of presenting the dharma. Everybody says their way is the best and things are further complicated by mixing the dharma with new-age spiritual teachings; the classical ones and the new ones are getting very mixed up. So that's why I believe that to bring this *Flight of Garuda* in Shabkarpa's own style—in a very simple, direct, bold way—is very, very important now. I chose to use very simple words in this translation, and to make it very accessible for students of these times.

I sincerely wish that this translation work and the teaching will benefit many people. The meaning of 'benefit' is that I hope people can understand what the organic nature of mind is and who we are. Today there are so many people struggling with emotional problems, mental toxins, ego, anger, stress, and addictions, so I think this *Flight of the Garuda* is very needed. It is very simple yet very deep. We can read and understand it in a simplistic way, but it is also very complex and sophisticated. That's why if somebody tells me, "I just want to read one book about meditation," I say, "Okay, read *Flight of Garuda*." One book for one lifetime: *Flight of Garuda*. Every year you read it, you have different understanding. Every month if you read it once, you can really have different insights.

And that's why I'm also happy that from this year in Arce, Italy Yuthok Ling we have started the 100-days *Flight of the Garuda* training, and we study it like the old style: we go out into nature as a group to meditate and to really make the practice very experiential and very personal.

I am very grateful to Tenzin Wainwright, who took my audio recordings, transcribed them, and dedicated his time and effort to compile this text. His work has fulfilled a long-held wish of mine. We have worked together on this for months and I'm impressed by his dedication.

My wish is that for experienced meditators this book will help them to dive deeply into their minds and realize the ultimate nature of mind. Medium-level yogis should find their knowledge and experiences confirmed by this book, bringing greater confidence. And then at least, I hope people can use this book as a tool for self-healing, particularly for psychological issues. Reading it, I hope, will heal our hearts and bring a sense of wholeness, safety, and spiritual connection with our own minds and emotions. May everyone who reads this book receive such blessings.

Dr. Nida Chenagtsang
Yuthok Ling, Arce 2025

༄༅། །ན་མོ་གུ་རུ་བྷྱཿ

NAMO GURU BHYA

Homage to all the gurus.

༄༅། །འོད་གསལ་རྫོགས་པ་ཆེན་པོའི་ཁྲེགས་ཆོད་ལྟ་བའི་གླུ་དབྱངས་ས་ལམ་མ་ལུས་མྱུར་དུ་བགྲོད་པའི་རྩལ་ལྡན་མཁའ་ལྡིང་གཤོག་རླབས་ཞེས་བྱ་བ་བཞུགས་སོ།།

ÖSEL DZOGPA CHENPÖ TREKCHÖ TAWÉ LU YANG SA
LAM MA LÜ NYUR DU DRÖ PÉ TSEL DEN KHADING
SHOKLAP ZHÉ JAWA ZHUK SO

The Song of the View of Trekchö, the Cutting Through of the Great Perfection of Clear Light, called "The Powerful Garuda's Wing Beats That Swiftly Traverse All Stages and Paths."

Introduction by Shabkarpa

།ཀུན་གསལ་མཁྱེན་བརྩེའི་ཏ་བདུན་དཀྱིལ་འཁོར་ལས།
།ཚད་མེད་ཐུགས་རྗེའི་འོད་ཟེར་རབ་སྤྲོས་ནས།
།ཁམས་གསུམ་འགྲོ་བའི་མ་རིག་མུན་པ་ཀུན།
།དུས་གཅིག་སེལ་མཛད་ཆོས་ཀྱི་རྒྱལ་པོར་འདུད།

KÜN SEL KHYEN TSÉ TA DÜN KYINKHOR LÉ
TSÉ MÉ TUK JÉ ÖZER RAP TRÖ NÉ
KHAM SUM DRO BÉ MA RIK MÜN PA KÜN
DÜ CHIK SEL DZÉ CHÖ KYI GYEL POR DÜL

Whose all-seeing mandala of wisdom and love, like the sun,
Radiates the immeasurable light rays of compassion
And instantaneously dispells the darkness of ignorance
of beings in the three realms,
I bow to the Dharma King, Chokyi Gyelpo.

།སྟོང་གསལ་ཆོས་སྐུའི་ལྷ་ལམ་ཡངས་པའི་དབྱིངས།
།བྱམས་དང་བརྩེ་བའི་རྒྱུ་འཛིན་རབ་འཁྲིགས་ནས།
།སྐལ་བར་ལྡན་པའི་གདུལ་བྱའི་འཛིན་མ་ལ།
།ཆོས་ཆར་འབེབས་མཁས་སྔགས་འཆང་རྡོ་རྗེར་འདུད།

TONG SEL CHÖ KÜ LHA LAM YANG PÉ NGÖ
JAM DANG TSEWÉ CHUNDZIN RAP TRIK NÉ
KELWAR DEN PÉ DÜL JÉ DZIN MA LA
CHÖ CHAR BEP KHÉ NGAKCHANG DORJÉ DÜ

In the vast sky of the empty and clear Dharmakaya
The clouds of love and compassion gather
Watering the earth of fortunate disciples
I bow to Ngakchang Dorje, who rains down the Dharma.

The Flight of Garuda

།ལྟ་བའི་གྲུ་དབུས་ལྷག་བསམ་དར་ཆེན་འཕྱར།
།བརྩོན་འགྲུས་རླུང་གིས་བསྐྱོད་ནས་སྲིད་མཚོ་རུ།
།བྱིངས་པའི་འགྲོ་རྣམས་སྐུ་གསུམ་ནོར་བུའི་གླིང་།
།འགོད་མཛད་དེད་དཔོན་འཇམ་དབྱངས་རྒྱ་མཚོར་འདུད།

TAWÉ DRU WÜ LHAK SAM DAR CHEN CHAR
TSÖN DRÜ LUNG GI KYÖ NÉ SI TSO RU
JING PÉ DRO NAM KU SUM NOR BÜ LING
GÖ DZÉ DÉ PÖN JAM YANG GYA TSOR DÜ

On the ship of the view, having hoisted the great banner
of pure intention,
And moved by the wind of diligence, across the ocean of existence,
I bow to Jamyang Gyatso, the captain who leads all beings to the
treasure island of the three kayas.

།དེ་གསུམ་མཁྱེན་བརྩེ་ཉི་བདུན་དཀྱིལ་འཁོར་ལས།
།འཕྲོས་པའི་བྱིན་རླབས་ནུས་མཐུའི་ཚ་བའི་ཟེར།
།སྐལ་ལྡན་བྱ་བཏང་པད་དཀར་བདག་ལ་ཕོག
།རིག་པའི་ཁ་བྱེ་ཉམས་རྟོགས་འདབ་སྟོང་བཞད།

DÉ SUM KHYEN TSÉ TA DÜN KYINKHOR LÉ
TRÖ PÉ JIN LAP NÜ TÜ TSAWÉ ZER
KEL DEN JA TANG PÉ KAR DAK LA POK
RIK PÉ KHA CHÉ NYAM TOK DAP TONG ZHÉ

The warming light-rays of the blessing power
Emanating from the wisdom sun of my three lamas
Touched this fortunate white lotus, and opened the bud of rigpa,
Causing a thousand petals of experience and realization to bloom.

Introduction by Shabkarpa

།བདག་བློའི་གེ་སར་སྟོ་བར་ལེགས་འཁྱིལ་བའི།
།ལྟ་བའི་གླུ་དབྱངས་མྱོང་གྲོལ་བདུད་རྩིའི་བཅུད།
།སྐལ་ལྡན་སློབ་མ་ཀང་དྲུག་ཚོགས་ལ་འབུལ།
།ངོམས་པ་མེད་པར་གུས་པའི་ཡིད་ཀྱིས་རོལ།།

DAK LÖ GÉ SAR TO BAR LEK KHYILWÉ
TAWÉ LU YANG NYONG DRÖL DÜ TSI CHÜ
KEL DEN LOP MA KANG DRUK TSOK LA BÜL
NGOM PA MÉ PAR GÜ PÉ YI KYI RÖL

Residing in the core of the open lotus flower of mind
Is the essence of the nectar of this song of the view,
which liberates by taste.
I offer it to the assembly of fortunate students,
like a swarm of bees
Enjoy it respectfully with insatiable minds.

The Flight of Garuda

SONG 1

What a Surprise!

༈ ཨེ་མ་ཧོ། བྱ་བཏང་གུ་ཡངས་ཡན་པ་བློ་བདེ་དངས།
EMAHO! CHA TANG GU YANG YEN PA LO DÉ NGÉ
Emaho! I'm a renunciate yogi, open minded, free and happy,

།ས་ལམ་མ་ལུས་མྱུར་དུ་བགྲོད་བྱེད་པའི།
SA LAM MA LÜ NYUR DU DRÖ JÉ PÉ
For all you who wish to swiftly traverse all the grounds and paths,

།ལྟ་བའི་གླུ་དབྱངས་མཁའ་ལྡིང་གཤོག་རླབས་ལེན།
TAWÉ LU YANG KHA DING SHOK LAP LEN
I sing this song of the view, like the wing beats of the garuda soaring in the sky.

།སྐལ་ལྡན་སེམས་ཀྱི་བུ་རྣམས་ལྷན་ནེར་ཉོན།
KEL DEN SEM KYI BU NAM LHEN NER NYÖN
Fortunate children of my heart, listen in a relaxed way!

།འཁོར་འདས་གཉིས་ལ་འབྲུག་གི་སྒྲ་བཞིན་དུ།
KHOR DÉ NYI LA DRUK GI DRA ZHIN DU
Like the sound of thunder, in both samsara and nirvana,

|ཡོངས་གྲགས་སངས་རྒྱས་ཟེར་བའི་སྒྲ་བོ་ཆེ།

YONG DRAK SANG GYÉ ZERWÉ DRA WO CHÉ
The great sound of "Buddha" is widely renowned.

|འགྲོ་དྲུག་སེམས་ཅན་རྒྱུད་ལ་རྟག་བཞུགས་ནས།

DRO DRUK SEM CHEN GYÜ LA TAK ZHUK NÉ
Abiding continuously in the minds of all sentient beings of the six realms,[1]

|སྐད་ཅིག་ཙམ་ཡང་གཡེལ་མེད་འགྲོགས་འདི་མཚར།

KÉ CHIK TSAM YANG YEL MÉ DROK DI TSAR
It accompanies us without separation, even for an instant – what a surprise!

|སངས་རྒྱས་རང་ལ་ཡོད་པར་མ་ཤེས་པར།

SANG GYÉ RANG LA YÖ PAR MA SHÉ PAR
Without knowing Buddha is within oneself,

|ཕྱི་རོལ་གཞན་དུ་སངས་རྒྱས་བཙལ་བ་མཚར།

CHI RÖL ZHEN DU SANG GYÉ TSELWA TSAR
It amazes me that one searches for Buddha outside.

|གསལ་དྭངས་ཉི་མའི་སྙིང་པོ་ཇི་བཞིན་དུ།

SEL DANG NYI MÉ NYING PO JI ZHIN DU
Just like the clear and radiant light of the sun,

|མངོན་སུམ་གསལ་ཀྱང་མཐོང་མཁན་ཉུང་བ་མཚར།

NGÖN SUM SEL KYANG TONG KHEN NYUNGWA TSAR
Even though it is bright and directly present, so few see it – what a surprise!

---

1. The Six Realms: Gods, Demi-Gods, Humans, Animals, Hungry Ghosts & Hell Realms

Song 1 - What a Surprise!

།ཕ་མ་མེད་པའི་རང་སེམས་སངས་རྒྱས་ཉིད།

PA MA MÉ PÉ RANG SEM SANG GYÉ NYI

One's own mind, the Buddha itself, without a mother and father,

།སྐྱེ་མ་མྱོང་ཞིང་འཆི་རྒྱུ་མེད་པ་མཚར།

KYÉ MA NYONG ZHING CHI GYU MÉ PA TSAR

Has never been born and will never die – what a surprise!

།བདེ་སྡུག་སྣ་ཚོགས་ཇི་ལྟར་མྱོང་ན་ཡང་།

DÉ DUK NATSOK JI TAR NYONG NA YANG

Whatever variety of happiness and suffering are experienced,

།བཟང་དང་ངན་དུ་ཆུང་ཟད་མི་འགྲོ་མཚར།

ZANG DANG NGEN DU CHUNG ZÉ MI DRO TSAR

It is not affected in the slightest for better or worse
– what a surprise!

།མ་སྐྱེས་གདོད་ནས་དག་པའི་སེམས་ཉིད་འདི།

MA KYÉ DÖ NI DAK PÉ SEM NYI DI

This very mind, unborn and primordially pure,

།མ་བཅོས་ཡེ་ནས་ལྷུན་གྱིས་གྲུབ་པ་མཚར།

MA CHÖ YÉ NÉ LHÜN GYI DRUP PA TSAR

Is spontaneously present from the beginning without any modification – what a surprise!

།རང་བཞིན་ཡེ་ནས་གྲོལ་བའི་རང་རིག་ཉིད།
RANG ZHIN YÉ NÉ DRÖLWÉ RANG RIK NYI
One's own awareness is naturally and originally free,

། གང་བྱུང་གང་དེར་བཞག་པས་གྲོལ་བ་མཚར།།
GANG JUNG GANG DER ZHAK PÉ DRÖLWA TSAR
Relax with how it is and liberation is there already – what a surprise!

SONG 2

Mind is the Essence of All Teachings

༈ ཨེ་མ་ཧོ། སྐལ་ལྡན་རིགས་ཀྱི་བུ་རྣམས་མ་ཡེངས་ཉོན། །
EMAHO! KAL DEN RIK KYI BU NAM LA MA YENG NYÖN
Emaho! Fortunate children of the lineage, listen without distraction!

དུས་གསུམ་རྒྱལ་བ་མ་ལུས་ཐམས་ཅད་ཀྱིས། །
DÜ SUM GYALWA MALÜ TAM CHÉ KYI
All the Buddhas of the three times, without exception,

ཆོས་ཕུང་བརྒྱད་ཁྲི་བཞི་སྟོང་ལ་སོགས་པའི། །
CHÖ PUNG GYÜ TRI ZHI TONG LASOKPÉ
Taught the 84,000 collections of Dharma and so forth.

གསུང་རབ་རྣམས་མཁའི་མཐའ་མཉམ་དཔག་མེད་ཀྱང་། །
SUNG RAB NAM KHÉ TA NYAM PAKMÉ KYANG
Even though the scriptures are immeasurable, like the expanse of the sky,

དོན་ལ་རང་སེམས་རྟོགས་ཕྱིར་གསུངས་པ་ལས། །
DÖN LA RANGSEM TOK CHIR SUNG PA LÉ
In essence, they were taught to realize one's own mind.

The Flight of Garuda

གཞན་དུ་ཅི་ཡང་རྒྱལ་བས་གསུངས་པ་མེད། །
SHENDU CHIYANG GYALWÉ SUNGPAMÉ
The Buddhas have not taught anything else.

དཔེར་ན་སྡོང་པོའི་རྩ་བ་གཅིག་བཅད་ན། །
PER NA DONGPÖ TSAWA CHIK CHÉ NA
For example, if you cut the main root of a tree,

ཡལ་ག་ལོ་མ་ཁྲི་འབུམ་དུས་གཅིག་བསྐམ། །
YALGA LOMA TRI BUM DÜ CHIK KAM
A hundred thousand branches and leaves will all dry up at once.

དེ་བཞིན་སེམས་ཀྱི་རྩ་བ་གཅིག་བཅད་ན། །
DEZHIN SEM KYI TSAWA CHIK CHÉ NA
Likewise, if you cut the single root of mind,

གཟུང་འཛིན་ལ་སོགས་འཁོར་བའི་ལོ་འདབས་བསྐམ། །
ZUNG ZIN LATSOK KHORWÉ LODAB KAM
The leaves of samsara, such as grasping at a projector and projection, will wither.

ཁང་སྟོང་མུན་པ་ལོ་སྟོང་ལོན་པ་ཡང་། །
KHANG TONG MÜNPA LO TONG LÖNPA YANG
Even the darkness of an empty room that has lasted for a thousand years,

སྒྲོན་མེ་སྐད་ཅིག་ཉིད་ལ་སེལ་བ་བཞིན། །
DRÖNMÉ KECHIK NYI LA SELWA ZHIN
Is dispelled by a lamp in just an instant.

Song 2 - Mind is the Essence of All Teachings

རང་སེམས་འོད་གསལ་རྟོགས་པའི་སྐད་ཅིག་ལ། །
RANGSEM ÖSAL TOKPÉ KECHIK LA
In the instant of realizing ones own mind's clear light,

བསྐལ་པ་གྲངས་མེད་བསགས་པའི་སྡིག་སྒྲིབ་དག །
KAL PA DRANGMÉ SAKPÉ DIKDRIB DAK
The karmic obscurations accumulated over countless eons are purified.

གསལ་དང་ཉི་མའི་སྙིང་པོའི་རང་བཞིན་དེ། །
SAL DANG NYIMÉ NYINGPÖ RANGSHIN DÉ
The nature of the clear and luminous sun,

བསྐལ་པ་སྟོང་གི་མུན་པས་སྒྲིབ་མི་ནུས། །
KALPA TONG GI MÜNPÉ DRIB MI NÜ
Cannot be obscured by the darkness of a thousand eons.

དེ་བཞིན་རང་སེམས་སྙིང་པོའི་འོད་གསལ་དེ། །
DEZHIN RANGSEM NYINGPÖ ÖSAL DÉ
Likewise, the clear light essence of your own mind,

བསྐལ་པར་འཁྲུལ་པས་སྒྲིབ་པར་མི་ནུས་སོ། །
KALPAR TRULPÉ DRIBPAR MI NÜ SO
Cannot be darkened by eons of delusion.

ནམ་མཁའི་རང་བཞིན་མདོག་དབྱིབས་ཚད་ལས་འདས། །
NAMKHÉ RANGSHIN DOK YIB TSÉ LÉ DÉ
The nature of the sky transcends color, shape, and limits.

དཀར་ནག་སྤྲིན་གྱིས་གོས་པར་མི་འགྱུར་ལྟར། །
KARNAK TRIN GYI GÖPAR MINGYUR TAR
Just as it doesn't change when covered by white or dark clouds,

The Flight of Garuda

སེམས་ཀྱི་རང་བཞིན་མདོག་དབྱིབས་ཚད་ལས་འདས། །
SEM KYI RANGSHIN DOK YIB TSÉ LÉ DÉ
The nature of mind transcends color, shape, and limits.

དགེ་སྡིག་དཀར་ནག་ཆོས་ཀྱིས་གོས་མི་འགྱུར། །
GEDIK KARNAK CHÖ KYI GÖ MINGYUR
It cannot be stained by good and bad actions.

དཔེར་ན་འོ་མ་མར་གྱི་རྒྱུ་ཡིན་ཀྱང་། །
PER NA OMA MAR GYI GYU YIN KYANG
For example, the origin of butter is milk.

མ་བསྲུབས་བར་དུ་མར་ནི་མི་འབྱུང་ལྟར། །
MATROKPAR DUMAR NI MINJUNG TAR
Until you churn the milk, you won't get butter.

འགྲོ་ཀུན་བདེར་གཤེགས་སྙིང་པོའི་རྒྱུ་ཡིན་ཀྱང་། །
DRO KÜN DER SHEK NYINGPÖ GYU YIN KYANG
Even though all beings have the origin of Buddha-ness,

ཉམས་སུ་མ་བླངས་སེམས་ཅན་སངས་མི་རྒྱས། །
NYAM SU MA LANG SEMCHEN SANG MA GYÉ
Without practice, sentient beings will not become Buddhas.

འདི་ཉིད་ཉམས་སུ་བླངས་ན་ཀུན་གྲོལ་ཏེ། །
DI NYI NYAM SU LANG NA KÜN DROL TÉ
Whoever meditates on just this will be liberated.

དབང་པོ་རྣམས་ལ་རྟོ་རྟུལ་ཁྱད་པར་མེད། །
WANGPO NAM LA NO TUL KHYEPAR MÉ
It doesn't matter if your mind is sharp or dull (smart or stupid),

Song 2 - Mind is the Essence of All Teachings

ཉམས་སུ་བླངས་ན་བ་གླང་རྫི་ཡང་གྲོལ། །
NYAM SU LANG NAWA LANG DZI YANG DROL
If you meditate on this, even a cow herder will be liberated.

མངོན་སུམ་རང་སེམས་འོད་གསལ་དོན་རྟོགས་ན། །
NGÖNSUM RANGSEM ÖSAL DÖN TOK NA
When you directly realize the meaning of your own mind's clear light,

ཁ་བཤད་མཁས་པ་འདི་ལ་མི་དགོས་ཏེ། །
KHA SHÉ KHEPA DI LA MI GÖ TÉ
You won't need eloquent explanations about it.

བུ་རམ་རང་གི་ཁ་རུ་ཟོས་པའི་ཚེ། །
BU RAM RANG GA KHA RU ZÖPÉ TSÉ
Just like when someone has tasted jaggery for themselves,

བུ་རམ་རོ་བཤད་མི་དགོས་ཇི་བཞིན་ནོ། །
BURAM RO SHÉ MI GÖ JIZHIN NO
They don't need the taste of jaggery explained to them.

འདི་ཉིད་མ་རྟོགས་པཎྜི་ཏ་ཡང་འཁྲུལ། །
DI NYI MA TOK PANDITA YANG TRUL
Without seeing the nature of mind, even great scholars get confused.

ཐེག་དགུའི་བཤད་པ་ཡོངས་ལ་མཁས་གྱུར་ཀྱང་། །
TEK GÜ SHÉPA YONG LA KHÉ GYUR KYANG
Even if they are expert in explaining all of the nine vehicles, [2]

---

2. The Nyingma school classifies the Buddhist path into nine vehicles: the Śrāvaka-yāna, Pratyekabuddha-yāna, and Bodhisattva-yāna (Three Sutra Vehicles); the Kriyā-tantra, Caryā-tantra, and Yoga-tantra (Three Outer Tantras); and Mahā Yoga, Anu Yoga, and Ati Yoga (Three Inner Tantras).

The Flight of Garuda

མ་མཐོང་རྒྱང་གི་གཏམ་རྒྱུད་བཤད་པ་བཞིན། །
MA TONG GYANG GI TAM GYÜ SHÉPA ZHIN
It's like telling a story from far away without actually knowing.

སངས་རྒྱས་ས་ལ་གནས་ས་བས་ཀྱང་རིང་། །
SANG GYÉ SA LA NAMSA BÉ KYANG RING
For them, the state of Buddhahood is further than the sky from the earth.

ཡང་དག་རང་སེམས་འོད་གསལ་མ་རྟོགས་ན། །
YANGDAK RANGSEM ÖSAL MA TOK NA
If you don't realize the organic clear light of your own mind,

བསྐལ་པའི་བར་དུ་ཚུལ་ཁྲིམས་བསྲུངས་པ་དང་། །
KALPÉ BARDU TSULTRIM SUNGWA DANG
Even if you keep moral discipline for eons,

ཡུན་རིང་བར་དུ་བཟོད་པ་བསྒོམས་བྱས་ཀྱང་།
YÜN RING BARDU ZÖ PA GOM JÉ KYANG
And even if you push yourself to meditate with patience for a long time,

ཁམས་གསུམ་འཁོར་བའི་གནས་ནས་མི་འཕགས་པས། །
KHAM SUM KHORWÉ NÉ NÉ MI PAK PÉ
You will not escape the cycle of suffering in the three realms of samsara.

དེའི་ཕྱིར་འབད་པས་སེམས་ཀྱི་རྩད་གཅོད་ཀྱིས།། །།
DÉ CHIR BEPÉ SEM KYI TSA CHÖD KYI
Therefore, apply your effort, and cut the root of your mind.

SONG 3

Cut the Root

ཧཱུྃ ཨེ་མ་ཧོ། ད་ཡང་སྐལ་ལྡན་བུ་མཆོག་ཀུན་གྱིས་ཉོན། །
EMAHO! DA YANG KALDEN BU CHOK KÜN GYI NYÖN
Emaho! Again, my beloved children, listen to me!

རང་གི་སེམས་ཀྱི་རྩ་བདར་མ་ཆོད་ན། །
RANG GI SEM KYI TSA DAR MA CHÖ NA
If you don't thoroughly investigate the root of your own mind,

དགེ་སྦྱོར་གང་བྱས་གནད་དུ་མི་འགྲོ་སྟེ། །
GEJOR GANG JÉ NÉ DU MIN DRO TÉ
Whatever virtuous practice you do will miss the point
(nothing will work on you).

དཔེར་ན་འབེན་ནི་དྲུང་དུ་བཞག་ནས་ཀྱང་། །
PER NA BEN NI DRUNG DU SHYAK NÉ KYANG
For example, if a target is placed right in front of you,

མདའ་ནི་ཐག་རིང་ཕྱོགས་སུ་འཕེན་དང་མཚུངས། །
DA NI TAKRING CHOK SU PEN DANG TSUNG
It's like shooting the arrow towards a distant place.

The Flight of Garuda

རྐུན་མ་རང་གི་ཁྱིམ་དུ་བཞག་ནས་ཀྱང་། །
KÜNMA RANG GI KHYI MADU SHYAK NÉ KYANG
Or, if a thief is in your own house,

ཚད་གཅོད་དྲག་པོ་ཕྱི་རུ་བྱེད་དང་མཚུངས། །
TSA CHÖD DRAKPO CHI RU JÉ DANG TSUNG
It's like conducting a fierce search outside.

འདྲེ་ནི་ཤར་སྟེའི་ཕྱོགས་སུ་བཞག་ནས་ཀྱང་། །
DRÉ NI SHAR GÖ CHOK SU SHYAK NÉ KYANG
Or, if an evil spirit is in the east direction,

གླུད་ནི་ནུབ་ཀྱི་ཕྱོགས་སུ་གཏོང་དང་མཚུངས། །
GLÜD NI NUB KYI CHOK SU TONG DANG TSUNG
It's like throwing a lü* for the north direction.

དབུལ་པོའི་བྱིད་རྡོ་གསེར་དུ་མ་ཤེས་པར། །
ULPÖ GYÉ DO SER DUMA SHÉ PAR
Or, it's like a poor person, not knowing that their fire stones are made of pure gold,

གཞན་ནས་སློང་མོ་བྱེད་པ་ཇི་བཞིན་ནོ། །
SHEN NÉ LONGMO JEPA JIZHIN NO
(Feeling they have nothing) they go around begging from others.

དེས་ན་རང་གི་སེམས་ཀྱི་རྩད་བཅད་རྣམས། །
DINA RANG GI SEM KYI TSÉ DAR NAM
So therefore, thoroughly investigate, and try to cut the root of your own mind.

---

* Evil spirit offering

Song 3 - Cut the Root

འདི་བཞིན་ཆོད་ཅིག་སྐལ་ལྡན་སྙིང་གི་བུ། །
DI ZHIN CHÖ CHIK KALDEN NYING GI BU
Settle this with complete certainty, fortunate child of my heart.

སེམས་ཞེས་བྱ་བའི་རིག་རིག་འགྱུ་འགྱུ་བོ། །
SEM ZHÉ JAWÉ RIK RIK GYU GYU WO
This thing called 'mind', which is aware and moving,

བདས་ན་མི་ཟིན་ཡལ་ཡལ་བན་བུན་པོ། །
DÉ NA MI ZIN YAL YAL BEN BÜN PO
If chased, it can't be caught, it's fleeting and indistinct.

བཞག་ན་མི་སྡོད་ཚུབ་ཚུབ་ཡེར་ཡེར་པོ། །
SHYAK NA MI DÖ TSUB TSUB YER YERPO
You try to place it, but it doesn't stay, it runs away and scatters everywhere.

འདི་ཞེས་མཚོན་མེད་སྟོང་པ་ཕྱང་ཆད་པོ། །
DI ZHÉ TSÖNMÉ TONGPA CHANG CHEPO
You can't point to it, to say 'This is my mind,' it seems both empty and pervasive.

བདེ་སྡུག་སྣ་ཚོགས་མྱོང་མཁན་རང་གི་སེམས། །
DEDUK NATSOK NYONG KHEN RANG GI SEM
Ones own mind, which experiences all variety of happiness and suffering,

དང་པོ་འདི་ནི་བྱུང་ས་གང་ནས་བྱུང་། །
DANGPO DI NI JUNG SA GANGNÉ JUNG
In the beginning, where did it come from?

The Flight of Garuda

ཕྱི་ཡི་སྣང་བ་རི་བྲག་ཆུ་ཤིང་དང་། །
CHI YI NANGWA RI DRAK CHUSHING DANG
Did it come from external appearances like mountains, rocks, water, or trees?

ནམ་མཁའི་རླུང་སོགས་བརྟེན་བཅས་རྟེན་མེད་པ། །
NAMKHÉ LUNG SOK TEN CHÉ TENMÉ PA
Did it come from the wind in the sky? Did it come through interdependence, or is it something independent?

གང་ལས་བྱུང་ངམ་འདྲི་ཞིང་རྩད་བདར་གཅོད། །
GANGLÉ JUNG NGAM DRI ZHING TSA DAR CHÖD
Where exactly is it coming from? Ask yourself and thoroughly investigate.

ཡང་ན་ཕ་མ་གཉིས་ཀྱི་ཁུ་ཁྲག་ལས། །
YANGNA PAMA NYI KYI KHU TRAK LÉ
Did it come from the egg and sperm of your parents?

བྱུང་ངམ་སྙམ་ན་ཇི་ལྟར་བྱུང་ཚུལ་དཔྱོད། །
JUNG NGAM NYAM NA JITAR JUNG TSUL CHÖ
If you think it is, again, analyze how it comes!

དེ་ལྟར་དཔྱད་པས་བྱུང་ས་མ་རྙེད་ཚེ། །
DETAR CHEPÉ JUNG SA MA NYÉ TSÉ
When, in that way, you investigate and don't find an origin,

བར་དུ་ད་ལྟ་རང་ལུས་སྟོད་སྨད་དང་། །
BARDU DA TA RANG LÜ TÖMÉ DANG
Then ask yourself, where exactly is your mind located now? Is it in your body? If so, is it in the upper, or lower parts?

Song 3 - Cut the Root

དབང་པོ་དོན་སྙིང་ལ་སོགས་གང་ལ་གནས། །
WANGPO DÖNNYING LASOK GANGLA NÉ
Does it reside in the organs? In the heart, or brain, and so forth?

སྙིང་ལ་གནས་ན་མགོ་མཇུག་གང་ན་གནས། །
NYING LA NÉ NA GOJUK GANG NA NÉ
If it resides in the heart, is it in the top or the bottom?

དབྱིབས་དང་ཁ་དོག་ལ་སོགས་ཇི་ལྟར་འདུག །
YIB DANG KHADOK LASOK JITAR DUK
How does it exist in terms of shape and color?

ལེགས་པར་དཔྱོད་ལ་གནས་ས་མ་རྙེད་ཚེ། །
LEKPAR CHÖ LA NESA MA NYÉ TSÉ
When you have exhausted your search and found no location,

ཐ་མར་འགྲོ་དུས་ཡུལ་གྱི་དབང་པོའི་སྒོ། །
TAMAR DRO DÜ YUL GYI WANGPÖ GO
Then, lastly, try to find where your mind goes when it moves.
Does it go out through the doors of the senses?

གང་ནས་འགྲོ་དང་ཕྱི་རོལ་ཡུལ་རྣམས་སུ། །
GANG NÉ DRO DANG CHIROL YUL NAM SU
Where does it go out?

ཡུད་ཙམ་ཉིད་ལ་སླེབས་པའི་དུས་དེ་རུ། །
YÜTSAM NYI LA LEBPÉ DÜ DÉ RU
In an outer location, your mind arrives instantly.

ལུས་ཀྱིས་ཕྱིན་ནམ་སེམས་ཉིད་ཁོ་ནས་ཕྱིན། །
LÜ KYI SA CHIN NAM SEMNYI KHO NÉ CHIN
Did the body go, or did only the mind go?

ལུས་སེམས་ཚོགས་པས་ཕྱིན་སོགས་རྩད་བདར་ཆོད། །
LÜ SEM TSOKPÉ CHIN SOK TSÉ DAR CHÖ
Thoroughly investigate whether the body and mind went together.

དེ་ཡང་ཉོན་མོངས་རྣམ་རྟོག་སྐྱེ་བའི་ཚེ། །
DEYANG NYÖNMONG NAMTOK KYEPÉ TSÉ
Furthermore, when afflictions and conceptual thoughts arise,

དང་པོ་གང་ནས་སྐྱེས་དང་ད་ལྟའི་དུས། །
DANGPO GANGNÉ KYÉ DANG DA TI DÜ
From where did they arise?

གང་ལ་གནས་དང་མདོག་དབྱིབས་ཨེ་འདུག་ལྟོས། །
GANGLA NÉ DANG DOK YIB É DUK TÖ
Where do they reside now? Do they have color and shape?

ཐ་མར་རང་སར་ཞི་ནས་ཡལ་བའི་ཚེ། །
TAMAR RANG SAR ZHINÉ YELWÉ TSÉ
When they subside in their own place and disappear,
where do they go?

གང་དུ་ཡལ་ནས་འགྲོ་སོགས་རྩད་བདར་ཆོད། །
GANGDU YAL NÉ DRO SOK TSÉ DAR CHÖ
Thoroughly investigate where they disappear and go.

འཆི་བའི་ཚེ་ན་ཇི་ལྟར་བྱས་ནས་འགྲོ། །
CHIWÉ TSÉ NA JITAR JÉ NÉ DRO
At the time of death, how will the mind travel?

ཞིབ་ཏུ་དཔྱོད་ལ་སྐྱེ་འཆི་འགྲོ་འོང་དང་། །
SHYIBTU CHÖ LA KYECHI DRO ONG DANG
Investigate thoroughly, birth and death, coming and going.

ངོས་བཟུང་བྲལ་བའི་སྟོང་སངས་བརྗོད་མེད་དུ། །
NGÖ ZUNG DRALWÉ TONG SANG JÖMÉ DU
Gain certainty that mind is unidentifiable, ungraspable, intangible, empty and clear.

ངེས་པར་གཏན་ལ་མ་ཕེབས་བར་དུ་དཔྱོད། །
NGEPAR TEN LA MAPEBWAR DU CHÖ
Until you've settled on that, examine!

གཞན་གྱིས་དཔེ་དང་ཁ་བཤད་སྐམ་པོ་ཡིས། །
SHEN GYI PÉ DANG KHA SHÉ KAMPO YI
By following others' examples (books) and dry words,

སྟོང་པ་ཉིད་ཡིན་ཟེར་བས་མི་ཕན་ཏེ། །
TONGPANYI YIN ZERWÉ MI PEN TÉ
Merely saying "It's emptiness" won't help.

དཔེར་ན་སྟག་ཡོད་ཟེར་བའི་ས་ཆ་རུ། །
PER NA TAK YÖ ZERWÉ SA CHA RU
For example, in a place where it's believed there is a tiger,

གཞན་གྱིས་སྟག་ནི་མེད་པར་བརྗོད་ན་ཡང་། །
SHEN GYI TAK NI MEPAR JÖ NA YANG
Even if others say there is no tiger there,

རང་ཉིད་དེ་ལ་ཡིད་ཆེས་མི་སྐྱེ་བར། །
RANGNYI DÉ LA YICHÉ MI KYEWAR
You yourself will not have complete trust in that,

The Flight of Garuda

ཡིད་གཉིས་ཐེ་ཚོམ་ཟ་བ་ཇི་བཞིན་ནོ། །
YINYI TETSOM ZAWA JIZHIN NO
You will be full of doubt and uncertainty.

རང་གི་སེམས་ཀྱི་རྩ་བ་རང་ཉིད་ཀྱིས། །
RANG GI SEM KYI TSAWA RANGNYI KYI
You must search for the root of your own mind, by yourself.

ཞིབ་ཏུ་དཔྱད་ནས་གཏན་ལ་ཕབ་པའི་ཚེ། །
SHYIBTU CHÉ NÉ TEN LA PABPÉ TSÉ
After having thoroughly searched, arrive at a firm decision, and settle the matter.

དཔེར་ན་སྟག་ཡོད་ཟེར་བའི་ལུང་པ་དེར། །
PER NA TAK YÖ ZERWÉ LUNGPA DER
For example, in that valley where people say there is a tiger,

རང་ཉིད་སོང་ནས་ཕུ་མདོ་ཐམས་ཅད་དུ། །
RANGNYI SONG NÉ PU DO TAMCHÉ DU
If you yourself go there and search from top to bottom,

སྟག་ནི་ཨེ་ཡོད་བརྟད་བདར་བཅད་གྱུར་ནས། །
TAK NI É YÖ TSÉ DAR CHÉ GYUR NÉ
Having definitively investigated whether there is a tiger or not,

མ་རྙེད་ཚེ་ན་རང་ཉིད་ཡིད་ཆེས་ཏེ། །
MA NYÉ TSÉ NA RANG NYIL YIR CHÉDÉ
When you don't find it, then you will have self-trust.

Song 3 - Cut the Root

ཕྱིན་ཆད་ས་དེར་སྟག་ཡོད་སྙམ་པ་ཡི། །
CHINCHÉ SA DER TAK YÖ NYAMPA YI
From then on, the thought that there is a tiger in that place,

ཡིད་གཉིས་ཐེ་ཚོམ་མེད་པ་ཇི་བཞིན་ནོ།། ॥
YINYI TETSOM MEPA JIZHIN NO
Will be without doubt or hesitation.
(Once you are really sure, you will never doubt again!)

SONG 4

Introduction to the Ground of Mind

༄། ཨེ་མ་ཧོ། ད་ཡང་སྐལ་ལྡན་བུ་རྣམས་ཚུར་ཉོན་དང་། །
EMAHO DA YANG KALDEN BU NAM TSUR NYÖN DANG
Emaho! Now you fortunate ones, listen here!

ཁྱེད་རྣམས་དེ་ལྟར་བརྟགས་ཤིང་དཔྱད་པའི་ཚེ། །
KHYÉ NAM DETAR TAK SHING CHEPÉ TSÉ
When you examine and investigate in this way,

སེམས་ཞེས་མཛུབ་མོ་བཙུགས་ནས་འདི་ཡིན་ཞེས། །
SEM ZHÉ DZUBMO TSUK NÉ DI YIN ZHÉ
Pointing with your finger, saying, "This is mind,"

དངོས་པོར་གྲུབ་པ་རྡུལ་ཙམ་མ་རྙེད་ཚེ། །
NGÖPOR DRUBPA DUL TSAM MA NYÉ TSÉ
When you don't find even an atom of anything established as a real thing,

མ་རྙེད་པ་དེ་རྙེད་པའི་མཆོག་ཡིན་ནོ། །
MANYEPA DÉ NYEPÉ CHOK YIN NO
That non-finding is the supreme finding.

Song 4 - Introduction to the Ground of Mind

དོ་སྐོལ་སེམས་ལ་དང་པོ་བྱུང་ས་མེད། །
OKOL SEM LA DANGPO JUNG SAMÉ
Our mind has no place of origin.

ཡེ་ནས་སྟོང་པས་རོ་བོ་རོས་གཟུང་མེད། །
YENÉ TONGPÉ NGOWO NGÖ ZUNGMÉ
From the very beginning, it is free (emptiness) so its essence cannot be identified.

བར་དུ་གནས་ས་དབྱིབས་དང་ཁ་དོག་མེད། །
BARDU NESA YIB DANG KHADOK MÉ
In the middle, it has no place of dwelling, no shape, and no color.

ཐ་མར་འགྲོར་མེད་འདིར་སོང་རྗེས་མེད་དེ། །
TAMAR DRORMÉ DIR SONG JEMÉ DÉ
In the end, it has no place to go, no trace of having gone.

འགྱུ་བ་སྟོང་འགྱུ་སྟོང་པ་སྟོང་སྣང་ཡིན། །
GYUWA TONG GYU TONGPA TONG NANG YIN
The motion is empty motion; the emptiness is empty appearance,

སེམས་ཉིད་འདི་ནི་དང་པོ་རྒྱུས་མ་བསྐྱེད། །
SEM NYI DI NI DANGPO GYÜ MA KYÉ
This very nature of mind was not produced by causes in the beginning,

ཐ་མ་ཕྱི་རོལ་རྐྱེན་གྱིས་འདི་མི་འཇིག །
TAMA CHIROL KYEN GYI DI MI JIK
In the end, it is not destroyed by external conditions,

27

The Flight of Garuda

འཕེལ་དང་འགྲིབ་དང་གང་སྟོང་འདི་ལ་མེད། །
PEL DANG DRIB DANG GANGTONG DI LAMÉ
It is unaffected by increasing and decreasing, or anything whatsoever.

འཁོར་འདས་ཡོངས་ལ་ཁྱབ་པས་ཕྱོགས་རིས་མེད། །
KHORDÉ YONG LA KHYABPÉ CHOK RIMÉ
It pervades all samsara and nirvana, so it is free from bias.

འདི་ཞེས་མི་མཚོན་ཅིར་ཡང་འགག་མེད་འཆར། །
DI ZHÉ MI TSÖN CHIRYANG GAKMÉ CHAR
It cannot be pointed to as "this," yet it arises without obstruction as everything.

ཅིར་ཡང་མ་གྲུབ་ཡོད་མེད་མཐའ་ལས་འདས། །
CHIRYANG MA DRUB YÖMÉ TA LÉ DÉ
Not established in any way, it transcends the extremes of existence and non-existence.

འགྲོ་འོང་མེད་ཅིང་སྐྱེ་འཆི་གསལ་འགྲིབ་མེད། །
DRO ONG MÉ CHING KYECHI SAL DRIBMÉ
It has no coming or going, no birth or death, no clarity or obscuration.

Song 4 - Introduction to the Ground of Mind

སེམས་ཀྱི་རང་བཞིན་དྲི་མེད་ཤེལ་གོང་བཞིན། །
SEM KYI RANGSHIN DRIMÉ SHELGONG ZHIN
The nature of mind is like a stainless crystal ball,

ངོ་བོ་སྟོང་པ་རང་བཞིན་གསལ་བ་དང་། །
NGOWO TONGPA RANGSHIN SALWA DANG
Its essence is free, its nature is luminous,

ཐུགས་རྗེ་འགགས་པ་མེད་པར་ས་ལེར་གནས། །
TUKJÉ GAKPA MEPAR SALER NÉ
And its loving quality (compassion) is unstoppable, pervasive, and vivid.

འཁོར་བའི་སྐྱོན་གྱིས་ཅི་ཡང་མ་གོས་ཏེ། །
KHORWÉ KYÖN GYI CHIYANG MA GÖ TÉ
Untainted by any of the faults of samsara,

སེམས་ཉིད་ཡེ་ནས་སངས་རྒྱས་ཡིན་པར་ངེས། །
SEMNYI YENÉ SANGYE YINPAR NGÉ
The nature of mind itself is Buddha from the very beginning.

འདི་ནི་གཞི་ཡི་སེམས་ཉིད་གནས་ལུགས་ཀྱི། །
DI NI ZHI YI SEM NYI NELUK KYI
This is the basis of one's own mind, the unchanging ground of mind,

རང་བཞིན་གཏན་ལ་ཕབ་པའི་རྡོ་སྟོད་དོ།། ॥
RANGSHIN TEN LA PABPÉ NGOTRÖ DO
This was the introduction confirming the originality of mind as the Buddha-mind.

SONG 5

Introduction to the Ground of Delusion

ཧཱུྃ་ཨེ་མ་ཧོ། ད་ཡང་སྐལ་ལྡན་སེམས་ཀྱི་བུ་རྣམས་ཉོན། །
EMAHO DA YANG KALDEN SEM KYI BU NAM NYÖN
Emaho! Now again, fortunate heart-children, listen!

དང་པོ་ཆོས་སྐུ་ཀུན་ཏུ་བཟང་པོ་ཡིས། །
DANGPO CHÖKU KUNTUZANGPO YI
In the beginning, the Dharmakaya Samantabhadra,

སྒོམ་པ་རྡུལ་ཙམ་མ་བྱས་གྲོལ་ཚུལ་དང་། །
GOMPA DUL TSAM MA JÉ DROL TSUL DANG
Attained liberation without having practiced even a little meditation,

འགྲོ་བ་རྡུག་གིས་མི་དགེ་སྡིག་པའི་ལས། །
DROWA DRUK GI MI GE DIK PÉ LÉ
And the beings of the six realms' unwholesome, evil deeds,

སྤུ་ཙམ་མ་བྱས་འཁོར་བར་འཁྱམས་ཚུལ་ནི། །
PU TSAM MA JÉ KHORWAR KHYAM TSUL NI
Without having done even a little bit, they wander in samsara as follows:

Song 5 - Introduction to the Ground of Delusion

ཡེ་ཐོག་དང་པོ་ཀུན་གྱི་སྔོན་རོལ་དུ། །
YÉ TOK DANGPO KÜN GYI NGÖN ROL DU
In the very beginning, before everything,

འཁོར་འདས་མིང་མེད་གདོད་མའི་གཞི་ལ་གནས། །
KHORDÉ MINGMÉ DÖMÉ ZHI LA NÉ
Samsara and nirvana were without names, abiding in the original ground.

དེ་དུས་རིག་པ་གཞི་ནས་འཕགས་ཚུལ་ནི། །
DEDÜ RIGPA ZHI NÉ PAK TSUL NI
At that time, the way awareness arose from the ground is like this:

ཤེལ་ལ་ཉི་ཕོག་རང་འོད་ཕྱིར་གསལ་ལྟར། །
SHEL LA NYI POK RANG Ö CHIR SAL TAR
Just as sunlight striking crystal causes its own light to shine forth,

རིག་པའི་ཡེ་ཤེས་སྲོག་རླུང་གིས་བསྐྱོད་ནས། །
RIGPÉ YESHE SOK LOONG GI KYÖ NÉ
The wisdom of awareness, stirred by the life-sustaining wind (*loong*),

གཞོན་ནུ་བུམ་པ་སྐུ་ཡི་རྒྱ་རལ་ཏེ། །
ZHÖNNU BUMPA KU YI GYA RAL TÉ
Unraveled the expanse of the youthful vase body,

ལྷུན་གྲུབ་འོད་གསལ་སྐུ་དང་ཡེ་ཤེས་ཀྱི། །
LHÜNDRUB ÖSAL KU DANG YESHE KYI
And the spontaneously accomplished kayas and wisdoms.

ཞིང་ཁམས་མཁའ་ལ་ཉི་ཤར་བཞིན་དུ་གསལ། །
ZHING KHAM KHA LA NYISHAR ZHINDU SAL
The buddha-fields were clear like the sun rising in the sky.

དེ་དུས་ཆོས་སྐུ་ཀུན་ཏུ་བཟང་པོ་ཡིས། །
DEDÜ CHÖKU KUNTUZANGPO YI
At that time, the Dharmakaya Samantabhadra,

རང་སྣང་ཡིན་པར་ཤེས་པས་སྐད་ཅིག་ལ། །
RANGNANG YINPAR SHEPÉ KECHIK LA
Knowing it to be self-appearance, in a single instant,

ཕྱིར་གསལ་སྐུ་དང་ཡེ་ཤེས་ནང་དུ་ཐིམ། །
CHIR SAL KU DANG YESHE NANG DU TIM
Dissolved the outwardly manifest kayas and wisdoms into inner clarity.

ཀ་དག་གདོད་མའི་གཞི་ལ་སངས་རྒྱས་སོ། །
KADAK DÖMÉ ZHI LA SANGYE SO
Thus, was fully awakened in the original pure ground.

འོ་སྐོལ་རྣམས་ཀྱིས་རང་བཞིན་ལྷུན་གྲུབ་ཀྱི། །
OKOL NAM KYI RANGSHIN LHÜNDRUB KYI
All of us, however, in the spontaneously accomplished nature,

སྣང་བ་རང་གདངས་ཡིན་པར་མ་ཤེས་པས། །
NANGWA RANG DANG YINPAR MASHEPÉ
Failed to recognize appearance as our own self-projection,

ཤེས་པ་དྲན་མེད་འཐོམ་མེ་བ་དེ་ཉིད། །
SHÉPA DRENMÉ TOM MÉ BA DENYI
And that very state of unaware, confused consciousness,

དེ་ལ་ལྷན་ཅིག་སྐྱེས་པའི་མ་རིག་ཟེར། །
DÉ LA LHENCHIK KYEPÉ MARIG ZER
Is called "Innate ignorance."

དེ་ནས་གཞི་སྣང་འོད་གསལ་དེ་ཉིད་ལ། །
DENÉ ZHI NANG ÖSAL DENYI LA
Then, without knowing its own ground clear light appearance,

གཉིས་སུ་འཛིན་པའི་ཤེས་པ་སྐྱེས་པ་དེ། །
NYISU DZINPÉ SHÉPA KYEPA DÉ
Dualistic consciousness arose,

ཀུན་ཏུ་བཏགས་པའི་མ་རིག་པ་ཞེས་ཟེར། །
KÜNTU TAKPÉ MARIGPA ZHÉ ZER
This is called "conceptual ignorance".

མ་རིག་གཉིས་འཛིན་སྦུབས་སུ་དེ་དུས་ཚུད། །
MA RIG NYI DZIN BUB SU DEDÜ TSÜ
At that time, we entered the capsule of dualistic ignorance.

དེ་ནས་བག་ཆགས་རིམ་བཞིན་རྒྱས་ནས་ཀྱང་། །
DENÉ BAKCHAK RIMZHIN GYÉ NÉ KYANG
Then, as habitual tendencies gradually developed and increased,

འཁོར་བའི་བྱ་བ་འདི་རྣམས་ཐམས་ཅད་བྱུང་། །
KHORWÉ JAWA DINAM TAMCHÉ JUNG
All these activities of samsara arose.

དེ་ནས་ཉོན་མོངས་དུག་གསུམ་དུག་ལྔ་དང་། །
DENÉ NYÖNMONG DUK SUM DUK NGA DANG
Then, the three kleshas [3], the five toxic emotions [4],

བརྒྱད་ཁྲི་བཞི་སྟོང་ལ་སོགས་རྒྱས་ནས་ཀྱང་། །
GYÉ TRI ZHI TONG LASOK GYÉ NÉ KYANG
And the eighty-four thousand afflictions increased.

འཁོར་བའི་གནས་སུ་ཛོ་ཆུའི་འཁྱུད་མོ་བཞིན། །
KHORWÉ NÉ SU ZOCHÜ KHYÜMO ZHIN
In the state of samsara, spinning like water stirred in a bucket (hamster wheel),

འཁོར་ཞིང་བདེ་སྡུག་ད་ལྟའི་བར་དུ་མྱངས། །
KHOR ZHING DEDUK DA TI BARDU NYANG
We have wandered, experiencing happiness and suffering up to now.

རྒྱས་པར་འདོད་ན་ཀུན་མཁྱེན་ཐེག་མཆོག་མཛོད། །
GYEPAR DÖ NA KÜNKHYEN TEK CHOK DZÖ
If you wish for further elaboration, then look to Longchenpa's 'Treasury of the Supreme Vehicle' [5]

---

3. The Three Kleshas: **Ignorance** (Confusion / Stupidity), **Attachment** (Desire / Craving) and **Aversion** (Anger / Hatred).

4. The Five Toxic Emotions (or Five Mental Poisons) include the Three Kleshas, plus: **Pride** (Toxic ego) and **Jealousy**.

5. Treasury of the Supreme Vehicle (ཐེག་མཆོག་མཛོད, *Tekchok Dzö*) is one of the 'Seven Treasuries' written by the 14th-century Nyingma master Longchen Rabjam.

Song 5 - Introduction to the Ground of Delusion

ཟབ་དོན་རྒྱ་མཚོའི་སྤྲིན་ཕུང་སོགས་ལ་ལྟོས། །
ZAB DÖN GYATSÖ TRIN PUNG SOK LA TÖ
And look to the "Ocean Clouds of the Profound Meaning", and so on.

ད་ནི་བླ་མའི་མན་ངག་ཟབ་མོ་ཡིས། །
DANI LAMÉ MENGAK ZABMO YI
Now, through the profound instructions of the guru,

འཁྲུལ་པའི་རང་མཚང་ཐམས་ཅད་རིག་ནས་ཀྱང་། །
TRULPÉ RANG TSANG TAMCHÉ RIK NÉ KYANG
Having recognized all the self-faults and flaws of delusion,

རང་སེམས་སངས་རྒྱས་རང་ངོ་མཐོང་བ་ཡིན། །
RANGSEM SANGYE RANG NGO TONGBA YIN
One sees one's own mind as Buddha.

གདོད་མའི་མགོན་པོའི་རང་ཞལ་མཇལ་བ་ཡིན། །
DÖMÉ GÖNPÖ RANG ZHAL JALWA YIN
One meets the face of the primordial protector.

ཀུན་ཏུ་བཟང་པོར་སྐལ་པ་མཉམ་པ་ཡིན། །
KUNTUZANGPO KALPA NYAMPA YIN
One shares the same fortune as Samantabhadra.

སྙིང་ནས་དགའ་བ་སྒོམས་ཤིག་སེམས་ཀྱི་བུ། །
NYING NÉ GAWA GOM SHIK SEM KYI BU
So, meditate with joy and gratitude, children of my heart!

འཁྲུལ་པ་གཏན་ལ་ཕབ་པའི་ངོ་སྤྲོད་དོ།། །།
TRULWA TEN LA PABPÉ NGOTRÖ DO
This is the introduction that establishes the ground of delusion.

SONG 6

Pointing out the Nature of Mind

ཧཱུྃ ཨེ་མ་ཧོ། །ད་ཡང་སྐལ་ལྡན་སྙིང་གི་བུ་རྣམས་ཉོན། །
EMAHO DA YANG KALDEN NYING GI BU NAM NYÖN
Emaho! Now again, listen, fortunate heart-children!

སེམས་ཞེས་བྱ་བའི་ཡོངས་གྲགས་གྲགས་བོ་ཆེ། །
SEM ZHÉ JAWÉ YONG DRAK DRAWO CHÉ
The great and famous thing called "Mind,"

ཡོད་ནི་གཅིག་ཀྱང་ཡོད་པ་མ་ཡིན་ཏེ། །
YÖ NI CHIK KYANG YÖPA MAYIN TÉ
Is not truly one thing that exists,

འབྱུང་ནི་འཁོར་འདས་བདེ་སྡུག་སྣ་ཚོགས་འབྱུང་། །
JUNG NI KHORDÉ DEDUK NATSOK JUNG
Yet from it, the various phenomena of samsara and nirvana, happiness and suffering, arise.

འདོད་ནི་ཐེག་པའི་རྣམ་གྲངས་མང་དུ་ཡོད། །
DÖ NI TEKPÉ NAMDRANG MANGDU YÖ
There are many different ideas (about what mind is) according to the various vehicles.

Song 6 - Pointing out the Nature of Mind

མིང་ནི་བསམ་གྱིས་མི་ཁྱབ་སོ་སོར་བཏགས། །
MING NI SAM GYI MI KHYAB SOSOR TAK
The names given are numerous and various.

སོ་སོ་སྐྱེ་བོ་རྣམས་ཀྱིས་ང་ཡང་ཟེར། །
SOSO KYEWO NAM KYI NGA YANG ZER
Ordinary people call it "I," or "Ego"

མུ་སྟེགས་ལ་ལས་བདག་ཅེས་མིང་དུ་བཏགས། །
MUTEK LA LÉ DAK CHÉ MING DU TAK
Some non-Buddhists call it "Self" or "Ātman."

ཉན་ཐོས་པ་ཡིས་གང་ཟག་བདག་མེད་ཟེར། །
NYENTÖ PA YI GANGZAK DAKMÉ ZER
Śrāvakās say it is the "Selflessness"

སེམས་ཙམ་པ་ཡིས་སེམས་ཞེས་མིང་དུ་བཏགས། །
SEM TSAM PA YI SEM ZHÉ MING DU TAK
Cittamatrins call it "Mind."

ལ་ལས་ཤེས་རབ་ཕ་རོལ་ཕྱིན་པ་ཟེར། །
LA LÉ SHERAB PAROL CHENPA ZER
Some call it "Prajñāpāramitā," transcendental wisdom.

ལ་ལས་བདེར་གཤེགས་སྙིང་པོ་མིང་དུ་བཏགས། །
LA LÉ DER SHEK NYINGPO MING DU TAK
Some call it "Tathāgatagarbha," "Sugatagarbha," "Buddha-nature."

ལ་ལས་ཕྱག་རྒྱ་ཆེན་པོ་མིང་དུ་བཏགས། །
LA LÉ CHAKGYA CHENPO MING DU TAK
Some call it "Mahāmudrā," the great seal, or great gesture.

The Flight of Garuda

ལ་ལས་དབུ་མ་ཞེས་པའི་མིང་དུ་བཏགས། །
LA LÉ UMA SHEPÉ MING DU TAK
Some call it "Madhyamaka," the middle way.

ལ་ལས་ཐིག་ལེ་ཉག་གཅིག་མིང་དུ་བཏགས། །
LA LÉ TIGLÉ NYAK CHIK MING DU TAK
Some call it "Eka Bindu," the single essence.

ལ་ལས་ཆོས་ཀྱི་དབྱིངས་ཞེས་མིང་དུ་བཏགས། །
LA LÉ CHÖ KYI YING ZHÉ MING DU TAK
Some call it "Dharmadhātu," the space of all phenomena.

ལ་ལས་ཀུན་གཞི་ཞེས་པ་མིང་དུ་བཏགས། །
LA LÉ KÜNZHI SHÉPA MING DU TAK
Some call it "Ālayavijñāna," the ground-of-all.

ལ་ལས་ཐ་མལ་ཤེས་པ་མིང་དུ་བཏགས། །
LA LÉ TAMAL SHÉPA MING DU TAK
Some call it "Ordinary Awareness."

མིང་ནི་བསམ་གྱིས་མི་ཁྱབ་ཅི་བཏགས་ཀྱང་། །
MING NI SAM GYI MI KHYAB CHI TAK KYANG
Though innumerable names are applied in various ways,

དོན་ལ་འདི་ཉིད་ཡིན་པས་ཤེས་པར་གྱིས། །
DÖN LA DI NYI YINPÉ SHÉPAR GYI
Know that in reality, it is just this:

ཁྱེད་རྣམས་སེམས་ཉིད་རང་སར་གློད་ལ་ཞོག །
KHYÉ NAM SEM NYI RANG SAR LÖ LA SHOK
Unleash the mind, let it relax in its own place.

Song 6 - Pointing out the Nature of Mind

བཞག་དུས་ཐ་མལ་ཤེས་པ་རྗེན་ནེ་བ། །
SHAK DÜ TAMAL SHÉPA JEN NEWA
When it is left as it is, ordinary awareness is fresh and naked,

བལྟས་པས་མཐོང་རྒྱུ་མེད་པའི་སལེ་བ། །
TEPÉ TONG GYU MEPÉ SALÉWA
It is clear, without anything to be seen by looking.

རིག་པ་མངོན་སུམ་སལེ་ཧྲིག་གེ་བ། །
RIGPA NGÖNSUM SALÉ HRIK GEWA
Awareness is directly present, vivid and bright.

ཅིར་ཡང་མ་གྲུབ་སྟོང་ཞིང་སེང་རེ་བ། །
CHIRYANG MA DRUB TONG ZHANG SENGÉ BA
Empty and spacious, not established in any way.

གསལ་སྟོང་གཉིས་སུ་མེད་པའི་ཡེ་རེ་བ། །
SALTONG NYI SU MEPÉ YÉ REWA
It is the original state of non-dual clarity and emptiness.

རྟག་པ་མ་ཡིན་ཅིར་ཡང་གྲུབ་པ་མེད། །
TAKPA MAYIN CHIRYANG DRUBPAMÉ
It is not permanent; it is not established as anything.

ཆད་པ་མ་ཡིན་ས་ལེ་ཧྲིག་གེ་བ། །
CHEPA MAYIN SALÉ HRIK GEWA
It is not nihilistic; it is vivid and bright.

གཅིག་པུ་མ་ཡིན་དུ་མ་རིག་ཅིང་གསལ། །
CHIKPU MAYIN DUMA RIK CHING SAL
It is not singular; many things are known and clear within it.

The Flight of Garuda

དུ་མ་མ་ཡིན་དབྱེར་མེད་རོ་གཅིག་པ། །
DUMA MAYIN YERMÉ RO CHIK PA
It is not multiple; it is undivided, of one taste.

གཞན་ན་མེད་དེ་རང་རིག་འདི་ཉིད་དོ། །
ZHEN NA MÉ DÉ RANGRIG DI NYI DO
It is not elsewhere; just this self-awareness it is.

སྙིང་དབུས་བཞུགས་པའི་གདོད་མའི་མགོན་པོའི་ཞལ། །
NYING Ü SHUKPÉ DÖMÉ GÖNPÖ SHAL
The face of the primordial protector (Samantabhadra),
dwelling in the heart's center,

མངོན་སུམ་ད་ལྟའི་དུས་འདིར་མཐོང་བ་ཡིན། །
NGÖNSUM DA TI DÜ DIR TONGPA YIN
Is directly seen, in this very moment.

འདི་དང་འབྲལ་མེད་གྱིས་ཤིག་སྙིང་གི་བུ། །
DI DANG DRALMÉ GYI SHIK NYING GI BU
Do not be separated from this, my heart-child!

འདི་མིན་གཞན་ལས་ལྷག་པ་སུས་འདོད་པ། །
DI MIN ZHEN LÉ LHAKPA SÜ DÖPA
Who would desire something more than this elsewhere?

གླང་པོ་རྙེད་ཀྱང་རྗེས་འཚོལ་ཇི་བཞིན་དུ། །
LANGPO NYÉ KYANG JÉ TSOL JIZHIN DU
Like someone who, having found an elephant, still searches
for its tracks,

Song 6 - Pointing out the Nature of Mind

སྟོང་གསུམ་ཐམས་ཅད་བཏགས་སུ་བཏགས་ན་ཡང་། །
TONGSUM TAMCHÉ TAK SU TAK NA YANG
Even if you searched throughout the entire Trichiliocosm [6],

སངས་རྒྱས་མིང་ཙམ་རྙེད་པར་མི་སྲིད་དོ། །
SANGYE MING TSAM NYEPAR MI SI DO
You could not possibly find more than the mere name of "Buddha" elsewhere.

དངོས་གཞིའི་གནས་ལུགས་དོན་གྱི་རོ་སྟོད་དོ།། ༎
NGÖZHI NELUK DÖN GYI NGOTRÖ DO
This is the actual pointing out instruction of the nature of mind.

---

6. The **Trichiliocosm** or "Three-thousandfold world system" (Sanskrit: *trisāhasra-mahāsāhasra-lokadhātu*, Tibetan: སྟོང་གསུམ་གྱི་འཇིག་རྟེན་ཁམས་) is a central concept in traditional Buddhist cosmology, particularly elaborated in the Abhidharma literature. It represents an unimaginably vast, yet structured, expanse of the universe.

SONG 7

You Know

ཧཱུྃ ཨེ་མ་ཧོ། ད་ཡང་རིགས་ཀྱི་བུ་རྣམས་ལེགས་པར་ཉོན། །
EMAHO DA YANG RIK KYI BU NAM LEKPAR NYÖN
Emaho! And now, you fortunate ones, listen closely again.

ད་ལྟའི་རང་རིག་རང་གསལ་འདི་ཉིད་ལ། །
DA TI RANGRIG RANGSAL DI NYI LA
In this very moment of your own self-knowing, self-luminous awareness,

སྐུ་གསུམ་ངོ་བོ་རང་བཞིན་ཐུགས་རྗེ་དང་། །
KU SUM NGOWO RANGSHIN TUKJÉ DANG
The three kayas: essence, nature, and compassion,

སྐུ་ལྔ་ཡེ་ཤེས་ལྔ་སོགས་ཐམས་ཅད་ཚང་། །
KU NGA YESHE NGA SOK TAMCHÉ TSANG
And the five kayas [7], five wisdoms [8], and everything else are all complete and perfect.

རིག་པའི་ངོ་བོ་ཁ་དོག་དབྱིབས་ལ་སོགས། །
RIGPÉ NGOWO KHADOK YIB LASOK
The essence of this awareness, free from colors, shapes, and so on,

Song 7 - You Know

ཅིར་ཡང་མ་གྲུབ་སྟོང་པ་ཆོས་ཀྱི་སྐུ། །
CHIRYANG MA DRUB TONGPA CHÖ KYI KU
Is not established as anything at all, it is emptiness; Dharmakaya (the body of space).

སྟོང་པའི་རང་དངས་གསལ་བ་ལོངས་སྐུ་འོ། །
TONGPÉ RANG DANG SALWA LONGKU O
The clear, radiant self-display of that emptiness is Sambhogakaya (the body of perfect enjoyment).

སྣ་ཚོགས་འཆར་གཞི་མ་འགག་སྤྲུལ་པའི་སྐུ། །
NATSOK CHAR ZHIMA GAK TRULPÉ KU
And the unceasing flow of all kinds of appearances is Nirmanakaya (the body of manifestation).

དེ་རྣམས་མཚོན་པའི་དཔེ་ནི་འདི་དང་འདྲ། །
DENAM TSÖNPÉ PÉ NI DI DANG DRA
To show this through an example, it's like this:

ཤེལ་གྱི་མེ་ལོང་ཆོས་ཀྱི་སྐུ་དང་མཚུངས། །
SHEL GYI MELONG CHÖ KYI KU DANG TSUNG
Dharmakaya is like a crystal mirror.

---

7. The Five Kayas: **Dharmakaya** (Space Body / Reality Body); **Sambhogakaya** (Enjoyment Body); **Nirmanakaya** (Emanation Body / Manifestation Body); **Svabhavikakaya** (Essence Body / Nature Body); **Abhisambodhikaya** (Body of Manifest Enlightenment).

8. The Five Wisdoms (Sanskrit: *Pañca-jñāna*): **Dharmadhātu Wisdom** (*Chöying Yeshe*); **Mirror-like Wisdom** (*Melöng Yeshe*); **Wisdom of Equality / Equanimity** (*Nyamnyi Yeshe*); **Discriminating Wisdom / Wisdom of Discernment** (*Soso Tokpé Yeshe*); **All-Accomplishing Wisdom** (*Ja Drub Yeshe*).

རང་བཞིན་དྭངས་ཤིང་གསལ་བས་ལོངས་སྐུ་མཚོན། །
RANGSHIN DANG SHING SALWÉ LONGKU TSÖN
Its nature being pure and clear represents the Sambhogakaya.

གཟུགས་བརྙན་འཆར་གཞི་མ་འགག་སྤྲུལ་སྐུའི་དཔེ། །
ZUKNYEN CHAR ZHIMA GAK TULKÜ PÉ
And the way reflections constantly arise within it is like the Nirmanakaya.

འགྲོ་རྣམས་སེམས་ཉིད་ཡེ་ནས་སྐུ་གསུམ་དུ། །
DRO NAM SEMNYI YENÉ KU SUM DU
From the very beginning, the mind of all beings is the three kayas,

གནས་པ་ཡིན་ཏེ་རང་ངོ་ཤེས་ནུས་ན། །
NEPA YIN TÉ RANG NGOSHÉ NÜ NA
It's always been that way. If they could only recognize their own nature,

འགྲོ་བ་རྣམས་ཀྱི་སྒོམ་པ་རྡུལ་ཙམ་ཡང་། །
DROWA NAM KYI GOMPA DUL TSAM YANG
They would not need to do even a moment of meditation.

བྱ་མི་དགོས་ཏེ་དུས་གཅིག་འཚང་རྒྱ་འོ། །
JA MI GÖ TÉ DÜ CHIK TSANG GYA O
Without doing anything, they would be awakened in an instant.

སྐུ་གསུམ་དོ་སྟོན་བ་དད་བསྟན་པ་ནི། །
KU SUM NGOTRÖ TADÉ TENPA NI
Now, these three kayas were introduced as being distinct,

དོན་ལ་དབྱིངས་གཅིག་མ་གཏོགས་ཐ་དད་དུ། །
DÖN LA YING CHIK MA TOK TADÉ DU
In reality, they are just different aspects of the same single expanse.

བཟུང་ནས་འཁྲུལ་པར་མ་འགྲོ་སྙིང་གི་བུ། །
ZUNG NÉ TRULPAR MA DRO NYING GI BU
So please, dear ones, don't grasp at them as being separate, or you'll get confused!

སྐུ་གསུམ་ཡེ་ནས་སྟོང་པ་ཀ་དག་སྟེ། །
KU SUM YENÉ TONGPA KADAK TÉ
The three kayas are empty from the start, pure from the beginning,

གསལ་སྟོང་ཟུང་འཇུག་ངོ་བོ་གཅིག་པ་རུ། །
SALTONG ZUNGJUK NGOWO CHIKPA RU
Their essence is a single, unified state: the union of clarity and emptiness.

ཤེས་པར་གྱིས་ལ་འཛིན་མེད་ངང་ལ་སྐྱོད། །
SHÉPAR GYI LA DZINMÉ NGANG LA CHÖ
Recognize this and maintain that state without fixation.

ངོ་བོ་རང་བཞིན་ཐུགས་རྗེ་གསུམ་པོ་ཡང་། །
NGOWO RANGSHIN TUKJÉ SUMPO YANG
Those three qualities of essence, nature, and compassion,

ཆོས་སྐུ་ལོངས་སྐུ་སྤྲུལ་སྐུ་གཉིས་དང་མཚུངས། །
CHÖKU LONGKU TULKU NYI DANG TSUNG
Resemble the Dharmakaya, Sambhogakaya, and Nirmanakaya.

The Flight of Garuda

གསུམ་ག་གསལ་སྟོང་ཟུང་འཇུག་ཆེན་པོ་རུ། །
SUMGA SALTONG ZUNGJUK CHENPO RU
Know all three as the great union of openness and luminosity.

ཤེས་པར་གྱིས་ལ་འཛིན་མེད་ངང་ལ་སྐྱོད། །
SHÉPAR GYI LA DZINMÉ NGANG LA CHÖ
Recognize this and maintain that state without fixation.

དེ་ཡང་རང་བྱུང་རིག་པའི་ཡེ་ཤེས་འདི། །
DEYANG RANGJUNG RIGPÉ YESHE DI
What's more, this self-arising wisdom of awareness,

ཅིར་ཡང་སྣང་བས་རྣམ་པར་སྣང་མཛད་སྐུ། །
CHIRYANG NANGWÉ NAMPAR NANGZÉ KU
Appearing as everything, it is the body of Vairochana.

འགྱུར་བ་མེད་པས་མི་བསྐྱོད་རྡོ་རྗེའི་སྐུ། །
GYURWA MEPÉ MIKYÖ DORJÉ KU
Being utterly unchanging, it's the body of Akshobhya.

མཐའ་དབུས་མེད་པས་སྣང་བ་མཐའ་ཡས་སྐུ། །
TA Ü MEPÉ NANGWA TAYÉ KU
Having no center or limits, it's the body of Amitabha.

མཆོག་དང་ཐུན་མོང་དངོས་གྲུབ་ཀུན་འབྱུང་བའི། །
CHOK DANG TÜNMONG NGÖDRUB KÜN JUNGWÉ
Being the source of all siddhis, both supreme and ordinary,

Song 7 - You Know

ནོར་བུ་འདྲ་བས་རིན་ཆེན་འབྱུང་ལྡན་སྐུ། །
NORBU DRAWÉ RINCHEN JUNGDEN KU
Like a wish-fulfilling jewel, it's the body of Ratnasambhava.

དོན་ཀུན་འགྲུབ་པས་དོན་ཡོད་གྲུབ་པའི་སྐུ། །
DÖN KÜN DRUBPÉ DÖN YÖ DRUBPÉ KU
Effortlessly accomplishing all that needs to be done,
it's the body of Amoghasiddhi.

དེ་རྣམས་རིག་པའི་རྩལ་ལས་ལོགས་ན་མེད། །
DENAM RIGPÉ TZAL LÉ LOK NAMÉ
All of these are nothing other than the display, the energy,
of awareness itself.

རིག་པའི་ཡེ་ཤེས་ངོ་བོ་མ་འགགས་པར། །
RIGPÉ YESHE NGOWO MAGAKPAR
The very essence of this awareness-wisdom is unceasing in nature,

མངོན་སུམ་གསལ་བས་མེ་ལོང་ཡེ་ཤེས་སོ། །
NGÖNSUM SALWÉ MELONG YESHE SO
Being vividly clear, like a mirror, it's 'Mirror-like Wisdom'.

ཀུན་ལ་ཁྱབ་པས་མཉམ་ཉིད་ཡེ་ཤེས་སོ། །
KÜN LA KHYABPÉ NYAMNYI YESHE SO
Pervading everything equally, it's the 'Wisdom of Equality'.

རྩལ་ལས་སྣ་ཚོགས་འཆར་བས་སོར་རྟོག་གོ །
TZAL LÉ NATSOK CHARWÉ SORTOK GO
As all variety of things arise from its energy,
it is 'Discriminating Wisdom'.

The Flight of Garuda

དོན་ཀུན་འགྲུབ་པས་བྱ་གྲུབ་ཡེ་ཤེས་སོ། །
DÖN KÜN DRUBPÉ CHATRUB YESHE SO
Effortlessly completing all that needs to be done,
it's 'All-accomplishing Wisdom'.

དེ་དག་རྣམས་ཀྱི་ངོ་བོ་ཀ་དག་ཏུ། །
DEDAK NAM KYI NGOWO KADAK TU
The innermost essence of all of these, in its original purity,

འདུས་པས་ཆོས་ཀྱི་དབྱིངས་ཀྱི་ཡེ་ཤེས་སོ། །
DÜPÉ CHÖ KYI YING KYI YESHE SO
Is the 'Wisdom of the Expanse of Reality', the Dharmadhatu.

དེ་རྣམས་ཐམས་ཅད་རང་གི་རིག་རྩལ་ལས། །
DENAM TAMCHÉ RANG GI RIG TZAL LÉ
All of these, without a single exception, arise from the energy of one's own awareness.

ལོགས་ན་གྲུབ་པ་རྡུལ་ཙམ་མེད་པ་འོ། །
LOK NA DRUBPA DUL TSAM MEPA O
They don't exist as separate from that, not even by an atom.

སྐུ་གསུམ་ངོ་བོ་རང་བཞིན་ཐུགས་རྗེ་དང་། །
KU SUM NGOWO RANGSHIN TUKJÉ DANG
So, the essence, nature, and loving compassion of the three kayas,

སྐུ་ལྔ་ཡེ་ཤེས་ལྔ་པོ་གཅིག་ཆར་དུ། །
KU NGA YESHE NGAPO CHIKCHAR DU
And the five kayas and the five wisdoms, all at once,

Song 7 - You Know

མངོན་སུམ་མཛུབ་མོ་བཙུགས་ནས་ངོ་སྤྲད་ན། །
NGÖNSUM DZUBMO TSUK NÉ NGO TRÉ NA
If we point them out directly with the finger of our own experience,

ད་ལྟའི་ཤེས་པ་བཟོ་བཅོས་མ་བྱས་པ། །
DA TI SHÉPA ZOCHÖ MACHÉPA
What we find is this simple knowing, completely unfabricated,

རྐྱེན་གྱིས་མ་བསྒྱུར་འཛིན་པས་མ་བསླད་པའི། །
KYEN GYI MA GYUR DZINPÉ MA LEPÉ
Not changed by conditions, not obscured by grasping,

རིག་པ་ས་ལེ་ཧྲིག་གེ་འདི་ཀ་ཡིན། །
RIGPA SALÉ HRIK GÉ DIKA YIN
Clear, bright awareness, right here and now,

དུས་གསུམ་སངས་རྒྱས་ཐམས་ཅད་འདི་ལས་བྱུང༌། །
DÜ SUM SANGYE TAMCHÉ DI LÉ JUNG
All Buddhas of past, present, and future arise from this.

འདི་ནི་དུས་གསུམ་སངས་རྒྱས་ཐུགས་ཡིན་པས། །
DI NI DÜ SUM SANGYE TUK YINPÉ
This is the very mind of the awakened ones.

འདི་དང་འབྲལ་མེད་གྱིས་ཤིག་སྐལ་ལྡན་ཀུན། །
DI DANG DRALMÉ GYI SHIK KALDEN KÜN
So, you fortunate ones, be inseparable from this!

མ་བཅོས་རང་གསལ་འདི་ཀ་ཡིན་པ་ལ། །
MACHÖ RANGSAL DIKA YINPA LA
Since without changing anything, it's right here and clear by itself,

རང་སེམས་སངས་རྒྱས་མ་མཐོང་ཅི་ལ་ཟེར། །
RANGSEM SANGYE MA TONG CHI LA ZER
How can you say, "I don't see my own mind as Buddha"?

འདི་ལ་བསྒོམ་རྒྱུ་ཅི་ཡང་མེད་པ་ལ། །
DI LA GOM GYU CHIYANG MEPA LA
Since there's absolutely nothing to do or meditate upon here,

བསྒོམ་རྒྱུ་མ་བྱུང་བྱ་བ་ཅི་ལ་ཟེར། །
GOM GYUMA JUNG JAWA CHI LA ZER
How can you say, "I can't meditate"?

རིག་པ་མངོན་སུམ་འདི་ཀ་ཡིན་པ་ལ། །
RIGPA NGÖNSUM DIKA YINPA LA
Since this itself is direct, naked awareness,

རང་སེམས་མ་རྙེད་བྱ་བ་ཅི་ལ་ཟེར། །
RANGSEM MA NYÉ JAWA CHI LA ZER
How can you say, "I can't find my mind"?

གསལ་ཧྲིག་རྒྱུན་ཆད་མེད་པ་འདི་ཀ་ཡིན། །
SAL HRIK GYÜN CHÉ MEPA DIKA YIN
Since this flow is unceasing and vividly clear,

སེམས་ངོ་མ་མཐོང་བྱ་བ་ཅི་ལ་ཟེར། །
SEM NGO MA TONG JAWA CHI LA ZER
How can you say, "I don't see the true face of my mind"?

འདི་ལ་བྱ་རྒྱུ་རྡུལ་ཙམ་མེད་པ་ལ། །
DI LAJA GYU DUL TSAM MEPA LA
Since there isn't even an atom of anything to do here,

Song 7 - You Know

བྱས་པས་མ་བྱུང་བྱ་བ་ཅི་ལ་ཟེར། །

JEPÉ MA JUNG JAWA CHI LA ZER

How can you say, "Nothing arises from my efforts"?

གནས་དང་མི་གནས་གཉིས་སུ་མེད་པ་ལ། །

NÉ DANG MI NÉ NYI SU MEPA LA

Since abiding and not abiding are not two different things here,

གནས་སུ་མ་བཏུབ་བྱ་བ་ཅི་ལ་ཟེར། །

NÉ SU MA TUB JAWA CHI LA ZER

What does it mean to say, "My mind can't remain in that state"?

རང་རིག་སྐུ་གསུམ་རྩོལ་མེད་ལྷུན་གྲུབ་ལ། །

RANGRIG KU SUM TSOLMÉ LHÜNDRUB LA

Since the three kayas, in their self-aware nature, are effortlessly self-perfected,

བསྒྲུབས་པས་མ་འགྲུབ་བྱ་བ་ཅི་ལ་ཟེར། །

DRUBPÉ MA DRUB JAWA CHI LA ZER

What does it mean to say, "I can't accomplish them through practice"?

བྱར་མེད་ཅོག་གིས་བཞག་པས་ཆོག་པ་ལ། །

CHARMÉ CHOK GI SHAKPÉ CHOKPA LA

Since simply leaving things as they are, without any modification, is enough,

དེ་ལ་མི་ནུས་བྱ་བ་ཅི་ལ་ཟེར། །

DÉ LA MI NÜ JAWA CHI LA ZER

What does it mean to say, "I can't do that"?

The Flight of Garuda

རྟོག་པ་ཤར་གྲོལ་དུས་མཉམ་ཡིན་པ་ལ། །
TOKPA SHARDROL DÜNYAM YINPA LA
Since the arising and the liberation of thoughts are simultaneous,

གཉེན་པོས་མ་བྱུང་བྱ་བ་ཅི་ལ་ཟེར། །
NYENPÖ MA JUNG JAWA CHI LA ZER
What does it mean to say, "I don't have the antidote"?

ད་ལྟའི་ཤེས་པ་འདི་ཀ་ཡིན་པ་ལ། །
DA TI SHÉPA DIKA YINPA LA
Since just this raw knowingness is it,

འདི་ལ་མི་ཤེས་བྱ་བ་ཅི་ལ་ཟེར།། །
DI LA MI SHÉ JAWA CHI LA ZER
How can you say, "I don't know this."?

SONG 8

Look Directly at Your Own Mind

ཧཱུྃ ཨེ་མ་ཧོ། ད་ཡང་སྐལ་ལྡན་བུ་རྣམས་གུས་པས་གསོན། །
EMAHO DA YANG KALDEN BU NAM GÜPÉ SÖN
Emaho! Hello fortunate people, listen here!

རང་སེམས་དངོས་མེད་ནམ་མཁའ་སྟོང་པ་འདྲ། །
RANGSEM NGÖMÉ NAMKHA TONGPA DRA
Your own mind is without substance, like the empty sky.

འདྲ་འམ་མི་འདྲ་སྐལ་ལྡན་བུ་རྣམས་ཀུན། །
DRA AM MI DRA KALDEN BU NAM KÜN
Whether it is like this or not, all fortunate children,

བལྟ་རུ་མེད་པའི་ཚུལ་དུ་རང་སེམས་ལ། །
TA RU MEPÉ TSUL DU RANGSEM LA
Look directly at your own mind in its unobservable nature.

ཅེར་གྱིས་ལྟོས་ལ་ཆམ་གྱིས་ཞོག་དང་ཤེས། །
CHER GYI TÖ LA CHAM GYI SHOK DANG SHÉ
Look intently, let it be naturally, and you will know.

The Flight of Garuda

སྟོང་པ་ཕྱང་ཆད་དག་ཀྱང་མ་ཡིན་པར། །
TONGPA CHANG CHÉ DAK KYANG MAYINPAR
It is not just a blank emptiness,

རང་རིག་ཡེ་ཤེས་ཡེ་ནས་གསལ་བར་རེས། །
RANGRIG YESHE YENÉ SALWAR NGÉ
Know with certainty that your own awareness and wisdom are primordially clear.

རང་བྱུང་རང་གསལ་ཉི་མའི་སྙིང་པོ་འདྲ། །
RANGJUNG RANGSAL NYIMÉ NYINGPO DRA
It's like the essence of the sunlight, self-arising and self-clear.

འདྲ་འམ་མི་འདྲ་རང་གི་སེམས་ཉིད་ལ། །
DRA AM MI DRA RANG GI SEMNYI LA
Whether it is like this or not, look intently at your own mind,

ཅེར་གྱིས་ལྟོས་ལ་ཕྱམ་གྱིས་ཞོག་དང་ཤེས། །
CHER GYI TÖ LA CHAM GYI SHOK DANG SHÉ
Look intently, let it be naturally, and you will know.

རྣམ་རྟོག་འགྱུ་དྲན་དངོས་བཟུང་མེད་པར་རེས། །
NAMTOK GYU DREN NGÖ ZUNG MEPAR NGÉ
Know with certainty that conceptual thoughts and wandering memories are ungraspable.

འགྱུ་བ་ངེས་མེད་བར་སྣང་བསེར་བུ་འདྲ། །
GYUWA NGÉME BAR NANG SER BU DRA
Their movement is uncertain, like a breeze in space.

Song 8 - Look Directly at Your Own Mind

འདྲ་འམ་མི་འདྲ་རང་གི་སེམས་ཉིད་ལ། །
DRA AM MI DRA RANG GI SEMNYI LA
Whether it is like this or not, look intently at your own mind.

ཅེར་གྱིས་ལྟོས་ལ་ཕྱམ་གྱིས་ཤོག་དང་ཤེས། །
CHER GYI TÖ LA CHAM GYI SHOK DANG SHÉ
Look intently, let it be naturally, and you will know.

ཅིར་སྣང་ཐམས་ཅད་རང་སྣང་ཡིན་པར་ངེས། །
CHIR NANG TAMCHÉ RANGNANG YINPAR NGÉ
Know with certainty that whatever appears is your own appearance.

གང་སྣང་ཐམས་ཅད་མེ་ལོང་གཟུགས་བརྙན་འདྲ། །
GANG NANG TAMCHÉ MELONG ZUKNYEN DRA
Whatever appears is like a reflection in a mirror.

འདྲ་འམ་མི་འདྲ་རང་གི་སེམས་ཉིད་ལ། །
DRA AM MI DRA RANG GI SEMNYI LA
Whether it is like this or not, look intently at your own mind.

ཅེར་གྱིས་ལྟོས་ལ་ཕྱམ་གྱིས་ཤོག་དང་ཤེས། །
CHER GYI TÖ LA CHAM GYI SHOK DANG SHÉ
Look intently, let it be naturally, and you will know.

སེམས་ལས་མ་གཏོགས་གཞན་ན་ཆོས་མེད་པས། །
SEM LÉ MA TOK SHEN NA CHÖ MEPÉ
Since there is no dharma other than mind,

ལྟ་བ་བལྟ་རྒྱུ་གཞན་ན་ཆོས་མེད་དོ། །
TAWA TA GYU SHEN NA CHÖMÉ DO
There is no object of view other than mind.

སེམས་ལས་མ་གཏོགས་གཞན་ན་ཆོས་མེད་པས། །
SEM LÉ MA TOK SHEN NA CHÖ MEPÉ
Since there is no dharma other than mind,

སྒོམ་པ་བསྒོམ་རྒྱུ་གཞན་ན་ཆོས་མེད་དོ། །
GOMPA GOM GYU SHEN NA CHÖMÉ DO
There is no object of meditation other than mind.

སེམས་ལས་མ་གཏོགས་གཞན་ན་ཆོས་མེད་པས། །
SEM LÉ MA TOK SHEN NA CHÖ MEPÉ
Since there is no dharma other than mind,

སྤྱོད་པ་སྤྱོད་རྒྱུ་གཞན་ན་ཆོས་མེད་དོ། །
CHÖPA CHÖ GYU SHEN NA CHÖMÉ DO
There is no object of action other than mind.

སེམས་ལས་མ་གཏོགས་གཞན་ན་ཆོས་མེད་པས། །
SEM LÉ MA TOK SHEN NA CHÖ MEPÉ
Since there is no dharma other than mind,

དམ་ཚིག་བསྲུང་རྒྱུ་གཞན་ན་ཆོས་མེད་དོ། །
DAMTSIK SUNG GYU SHEN NA CHÖMÉ DO
There is no samaya to keep other than mind.

སེམས་ལས་མ་གཏོགས་གཞན་ན་ཆོས་མེད་པས། །
SEM LÉ MA TOK SHEN NA CHÖ MEPÉ
Since there is no dharma other than mind,

Song 8 - Look Directly at Your Own Mind

འབྲས་བུ་བསྒྲུབ་རྒྱུ་གཞན་ན་ཆོས་མེད་དོ། །
DREBU DRUB GYU SHEN NA CHÖMÉ DO
There is no result to be achieved other than mind.

ཡང་ལྟོས་ཡང་ལྟོས་རང་གི་སེམས་ལ་ལྟོས། །
YANG TÖ YANG TÖ RANG GI SEM LA TÖ
Look again and again, look at your own mind!

ཕྱི་རོལ་ནམ་མཁའི་ཁམས་ལ་སེམས་གཏོང་ལ། །
CHIROL NAMKHÉ KHAM LA SEM TONG LA
Release your mind into the expanse of space,

རང་སེམས་ཉིད་ལ་འགྲོ་འོང་ཨེ་འདུག་ལྟོས། །
RANGSEM NYI LA DRO ONG É DUK TÖ
Look to see if your own mind has any coming or going.

བལྟས་ཚེ་འགྲོ་འོང་སེམས་ལ་མི་གདའ་ན། །
TÉ TSÉ DRO ONG SEM LA MI DA NA
When you see there is no coming or going in the mind,

ནང་གི་རང་གི་སེམས་ལ་ཚུར་བལྟས་ལ། །
NANG GI RANG GI SEM LA TSUR TÉ LA
Look backwards at your own mind within.

རྟོག་པ་འཕྲོ་བའི་འཕྲོ་མཁན་ཨེ་འདུག་ལྟོས། །
TOKPA TROWÉ TRO KHEN É DUK TÖ
Look to see if there is a "thinker" who generates thoughts.

རྟོག་པ་འཕྲོ་བའི་འཕྲོ་མཁན་མི་གདའ་ན། །
TOKPA TROWÉ TRO KHEN MI DA NA
If you see there is no thinker who generates thoughts,

སེམས་ལ་ཁ་དོག་དབྱིབས་སོགས་ཨེ་འདུག་ལྟོས། །
SEM LAKHA DOK YIB SOK É DUK TÖ
Look to see if the mind has a color or shape.

ཁ་དོག་དབྱིབས་མེད་སྟོང་པར་ཐུག་པའི་ཚེ། །
KHADOK YIBMÉ TONGPAR TUKPÉ TSÉ
When you find it to be empty, without color or shape,

སྟོང་པ་ཉིད་ལ་མཐའ་དབུས་ཨེ་འདུག་ལྟོས། །
TONGPANYI LA TA Ü É DUK TÖ
Look to see if that emptiness has a center and edge.

མཐའ་དབུས་མེད་ཚེ་ཕྱི་ནང་ཨེ་འདུག་ལྟོས། །
TA ÜMÉ TSÉ CHINANG É DUK TÖ
If there is no center or edge, look to see if there is an inside or outside.

ཕྱི་དང་ནང་མེད་རིག་པ་མཁའ་ལྟར་ཡངས། །
CHI DANG NANGMÉ RIGPA KHA TAR YANG
Without inside or outside, awareness is vast like the sky.

ཟང་ངེ་ཐལ་ལེར་རྒྱ་ཆད་ཕྱོགས་ལྷུང་བྲལ། །
ZANG NGÉ TAL LER GYACHÉ CHOK LHUNG DRAL
Clear, open, lucid, without limits, without taking sides.

རང་རིག་ཁྱབ་གདལ་ཀློང་ཆེན་ཡངས་པའི་དང་། །
RANGRIG KHYAB DAL LONGCHEN YANGPÉ NGANG
In the state of your own pervasive, vast and spacious awareness,

Song 8 - Look Directly at Your Own Mind

འཁོར་འདས་ཆོས་རྣམས་བར་སྣང་འཇའ་ཚོན་བཞིན། །
KHORDÉ CHÖ NAM BAR NANG JATSÖN ZHIN
All the phenomena of samsara and nirvana are like rainbows in the sky.

སྣ་ཚོགས་སྣང་ཡང་སེམས་ཀྱི་རོལ་པ་སྟེ། །
NATSOK NANG YANG SEM KYI ROLPA TÉ
Though various appearances occur, they are the play of the mind.

རང་རིག་གཡོ་མེད་ངང་ལས་ཕར་ལྟོས་དང་། །
RANGRIG YOMÉ NGANG LÉ PAR TÖ DANG
Look from the state of your own unmoving awareness.

ཆོས་རྣམས་ཐམས་ཅད་སྒྱུ་མ་ཆུ་ཟླ་བཞིན། །
CHÖ NAM TAMCHÉ GYUMA CHUDA ZHIN
All phenomena are like illusions or the moon in water.

སྣང་སྟོང་སོ་སོར་དབྱེ་བར་མི་ནུས་སོ། །
NANGTONG SOSOR YEWAR MI NÜ SO
Appearance and emptiness cannot be separated.

རིག་པའི་ངང་ལ་འཁོར་འདས་གཉིས་སུ་མེད། །
RIGPÉ NGANG LA KHORDÉ NYISUMÉ
In the state of awareness, samsara and nirvana are non-dual.

རང་རིག་གཡོ་མེད་ངང་ནས་ཕར་ལྟོས་དང་། །
RANGRIG YOMÉ NGANG NÉ PAR TÖ DANG
Look from the state of your own unmoving awareness.

འཁོར་འདས་ཆོས་རྣམས་མེ་ལོང་གཟུགས་བརྙན་བཞིན། །
KHORDÉ CHÖ NAM MELONG ZUKNYEN ZHIN
All the phenomena of samsara and nirvana are like reflections in a mirror.

ཇི་ལྟར་སྣང་ཡང་གདོད་ནས་ཡོད་མ་མྱོང༌། །
JITAR NANG YANG DÖNÉ YÖ MA NYONG
Whatever way they appear, they have never existed from the beginning.

འཁོར་འདས་མིང་མེད་ཐམས་ཅད་ཆོས་སྐུ་ཡིན། །
KHORDÉ MINGMÉ TAMCHÉ CHÖKU YIN
There is no name of samsara and nirvana, all are the Dharmakaya.

ཁམས་གསུམ་འཁོར་བར་འཁྱམས་པའི་འགྲོ་ཀུན་གྱིས། །
KHAM SUM KHORWAR KHYAMPÉ DRO KÜN GYI
All beings wandering in the three realms of samsara,

ཡེ་ནས་འཁོར་འདས་ཆོས་ཀུན་མཉམ་ཉིད་དུ། །
YENÉ KHORDÉ CHÖ KÜN NYAMNYI DU
Though primordially all phenomena of samsara and nirvana are equal,

གནས་པའི་ཡེ་ཤེས་རང་ངོ་མ་རྟོགས་པར། །
NÉ PÉ YESHE RANG NGO MATOKPAR
Abiding in wisdom, they fail to realize their own nature.

གཉིས་འཛིན་འཁྲུལ་པའི་དབང་གིས་སོ་སོར་བཟུང༌། །
NYIDZIN TRULPÉ WANG GI SOSOR ZUNG
Due to the power of dualistic delusion, they grasp this as separate.

Song 8 - Look Directly at Your Own Mind

གཉིས་མེད་དོན་ལ་གཉིས་འཛིན་ཕྱིར་མ་གྲོལ། །
NYIMÉ DÖN LA NYIDZIN CHIR MA DROL
Because of dualistic grasping, one is not liberated into the non-dual reality.

ཀུན་གྱིས་རང་སེམས་འཁོར་འདས་དབྱེར་མེད་ལ། །
KÜN GYI RANGSEM KHORDÉ YERMÉ LA
Everyone's own mind, which is nondual with samsara and nirvana,

སྤང་བླང་འདོར་ལེན་བྱས་པས་འཁོར་བར་འཁྱམས། །
PANGLANG DOR LEN JEPÉ KHORWAR KHYAM
Wanders in samsara by accepting and rejecting, receiving and refusing.

རང་རིག་སྐུ་གསུམ་རྩོལ་མེད་ལྷུན་གྲུབ་ལས། །
RANGRIG KU SUM TSOLMÉ LHÜNDRUB LÉ
From one's own awareness, the three kayas are spontaneously accomplished without effort.

འདི་མིན་ཐག་རིང་གཞན་དུ་འགྲོ་ཐབས་ཀྱིས། །
DI MIN TAKRING SHENDU DRO TAB KYI
By trying to get somewhere else, far away from this,

ས་ལམ་བཙལ་ནས་བླུན་རྨོངས་འགྲོ་བ་ཀུན། །
SALAM TSAL NÉ LÜN MONG DROWA KÜN
By searching for paths and stages, all foolish and ignorant beings,

སངས་རྒྱས་ས་ལ་སླེབས་པའི་དུས་མ་བྱུང་། །
SANGYE SA LA LEBPÉ DÜ MA JUNG
Have not reached the state of Buddhahood.

གང་སྣང་ཐམས་ཅད་རང་སྣང་ཡིན་པར་དེས། །
GANG NANG TAMCHÉ RANGNANG YINPAR NGÉ
Know with certainty that whatever appears
is your own appearance.

རང་རིག་གཡོ་མེད་ངང་ནས་ཕར་ལྟོས་དང་། །
RANGRIG YOMÉ NGANG NÉ PAR TÖ DANG
Look from the state of your own unmoving awareness.

སྣང་ཞིང་སྲིད་པ་ཐམས་ཅད་གཟུགས་བརྙན་འདྲ། །
NANG ZHING SIPA TAMCHÉ ZUKNYEN DRA
All appearance and existence are like reflections.

སྣང་སྟོང་གྲག་སྟོང་རང་བཞིན་ཡེ་ནས་སྟོང་། །
NANGTONG DRAK TONG RANGSHIN YENÉ TONG
Appearance is empty, sound is empty, their nature is
primordially empty.

དེ་ལྟར་བལྟ་མཁན་སེམས་ལ་ཚུར་ལྟོས་དང་། །
DETAR TA KHEN SEM LA TSUR TÖ DANG
Look back at the mind that is looking in that way.

དྲན་རྟོག་རང་ཡལ་སྟོང་པ་ནམ་མཁའ་འདྲ། །
DREN TOK RANG YAL TONGPA NAMKHA DRA
Memories and thoughts disappear by themselves,
empty like the sky.

སྤྲོས་མེད་སྤྲོས་བྲལ་བླ་བསམ་བརྗོད་ལས་འདས། །
TRÖMÉ TRÖDRAL MA SAM JÖ LÉ DÉ
It is clear without fabrication, beyond words, thought,
and expression.

Song 8 - Look Directly at Your Own Mind

གང་སྣང་ཐམས་ཅད་སེམས་ཀྱིས་ཆོ་འཕྲུལ་ཏེ། །
GANG NANG TAMCHÉ SEM KYI CHOTRUL TÉ
Whatever appears is the magic of the mind.

ཆོ་འཕྲུལ་ཐམས་ཅད་གཞི་མེད་སྟོང་པ་ཡིན། །
CHOTRUL TAMCHÉ SHYIMÉ TONGPA YIN
All magic is baseless and empty.

ཐམས་ཅད་རང་གི་སེམས་སུ་རྟོགས་གྱུར་ན། །
TAMCHÉ RANG GI SEM SU TOK GYUR NA
When you realize everything as your own mind,

མཐོང་སྣང་ཐམས་ཅད་སྟོང་པ་ཆོས་སྐུ་ཡིན། །
TONG NANG TAMCHÉ TONGPA CHÖKU YIN
All that is seen is the empty Dharmakaya.

སྣང་བས་མི་འཆིང་ཞེན་པས་འཆིང་བ་ཡིན། །
NANGWÉ MI CHING SHENPÉ CHINGWA YIN
Appearances do not bind, but attachment does.

ཞེན་ཆགས་འཁྲུལ་པ་ཆོད་ཅིག་སྙིང་གི་བུ།། །།
SHEN CHAK TRULWA CHÖ CHIK NYING GI BU
So, cut through the delusion of toxic attachment, child of my heart!

SONG 9

Magic Projection

ཧྰོ ཨེ་མ་ཧོ། སྐལ་བར་ལྡན་པའི་སེམས་ཀྱི་བུ་མཆོག་རྣམས། །
EMAHO KALWAR DENPÉ SEM KYI BU CHOK NAM
Emaho! Fortunate, supreme children of my heart.

ལྕག་གིས་མ་བརྒྱབ་རྟ་ལ་བང་མི་ལྡང་། །
CHAK GI MA GYAB TA LA BANG MI DANG
If you don't whip a horse, it won't run fast.

མང་དུ་མ་བསྲུབས་འོ་མར་མར་མི་ཆགས། །
MANGDU MA SUB OMAR MAR MI CHAK
If you don't churn the milk, butter won't form.

ཞིབ་ཏུ་མ་བཤད་གཏན་ལ་མི་ཕེབས་པས། །
SHYIBTU MA SHÉ TEN LA MI PEBPÉ
Since without explaining in detail, you won't understand,

ཚིག་ཁ་མང་པོའི་གླུ་དབྱངས་ལེན་པ་ལ། །
TSIK KHA MANGPÖ LUYANG LENPA LA
Whilst I sing this song of many words,

Song 9 - Magic Projection

སྣང་བ་མ་སུན་དགའ་བའི་སེམས་ཀྱིས་ཉོན། །
NANGWA MA SÜN GAWÉ SEM KYI NYÖN
Don't get bored, listen with a happy mind!

སྣང་བ་ཐམས་ཅད་སེམས་སུ་མ་ཤེས་ན། །
NANGWA TAMCHÉ SEM SU MA SHÉ NA
If you don't understand all appearances as mind,

སྟོང་ཉིད་དོན་དེ་ནམ་ཡང་མི་རྟོགས་པས། །
TONGNYI DÖN DÉ NAMYANG MI TOKPÉ
You will never realize the meaning of emptiness.

སྣང་བ་འདི་དག་དང་པོ་གང་ལས་བྱུང་། །
NANGWA DIDAK DANGPO GANGLÉ JUNG
Where did these appearances come from in the beginning?

བར་དུ་གར་གནས་ཐ་མ་གང་དུ་འགྲོ། །
BARDU GAR NÉ TAMA GANGDU DRO
Where do they abide in the middle, and where do they go in the end?

སྐལ་ལྡན་བུ་ཀུན་ལེགས་པར་རྟོག་དཔྱོད་གཏོངས། །
KALDEN BU KÜN LEKPAR TOKCHÖ TONG
All fortunate ones, please investigate well.

བརྟགས་ཚེ་དཔེར་ན་ནམ་མཁའི་ན་བུན་དེ། །
TAK TSÉ PER NA NAMKHÉ NABÜN DÉ
When you investigate, for example, a fog in the sky,

མཁའ་ལས་བྱུང་ཞིང་སླར་ཡང་མཁའ་ལ་འགྲོ། །
KHA LÉ JUNG ZHING LAR YANG KHA LA DRO
It arises from the sky and again goes back into the sky.

The Flight of Garuda

དེ་བཞིན་སྣང་བ་སེམས་ཀྱི་ཆོ་འཕྲུལ་ཏེ། །
DEZHIN NANGWA SEM KYI CHOTRUL TÉ
Likewise, appearances are the magic of the mind.

རང་གི་སེམས་སུ་ཤར་ཞིང་སེམས་སུ་འགྲོ། །
RANG GI SEM SU SHAR ZHING SEM SU DRO
They arise in your own mind and go back into the mind.

དཔེར་ན་མིག་གི་དབང་པོ་བསླད་པའི་མིས། །
PER NA MIK GI WANGPO LEPÉ MI
For example, a person whose sense of sight is impaired,

བར་སྣང་ཁམས་བལྟས་རབ་རིབ་སྣང་བ་དེ། །
BAR NANG KHAM TÉ RABRIB NANGWA DÉ
Looks at the sky and sees a shimmering appearance.

ནམ་མཁར་ཡོད་ཡོད་འདྲ་བར་སྣང་ན་ཡང་། །
NAMKHAR YÖ YÖ DRA BAR NANG NA YANG
Even though the shimmer appears as if it exists in the sky,

མཁའ་ལ་མེད་དེ་མིག་གི་ཆོ་འཕྲུལ་ཡིན། །
KHA LAMÉ DÉ MIK GI CHOTRUL YIN
It is not in the sky; it is the magic of the eye.

དེ་བཞིན་དངོས་འཛིན་བག་ཆགས་ངན་པ་ཡིས། །
DEZHIN NGÖDZIN BAKCHAK NGENPA YI
Likewise, due to the negative habitual tendency
of grasping at reality,

སེམས་ཀྱི་དབང་པོ་བསླད་པའི་མཐུ་ཡིས་ནི། །
SEM KYI WANGPO LEPÉ TU YI NI
Through the power of the pollution of mind,

Song 9 - Magic Projection

ཀུན་རྫོབ་སྣང་གྲག་ཆོས་རྣམས་ཐམས་ཅད་ཀུན། །
KÜNDZOB NANG DRAK CHÖ NAM TAMCHÉ KÜN
All the phenomena of relative appearance and sound,

བདེན་པར་ཡོད་ཡོད་འདྲ་བར་སྣང་ན་ཡང་། །
DENPAR YÖ YÖ DRA BAR NANG NA YANG
Even though appearing as if they truly exist,

གདོད་ནས་དངོས་པོར་གྲུབ་པ་རྡུལ་ཙམ་ཡང་། །
DÖNÉ NGÖPOR DRUBPA DUL TSAM YANG
From the beginning, not even an atom is established as truly existent.

མེད་དེ་རང་གི་སེམས་ཀྱི་ཆོ་འཕྲུལ་ཡིན། །
MÉ DÉ RANG GI SEM KYI CHOTRUL YIN
They do not exist; it is the magic of your own mind.

ཆོ་འཕྲུལ་ཐམས་ཅད་གཞི་མེད་སྟོང་པ་ཡིན། །
CHOTRUL TAMCHÉ SHYIMÉ TONGPA YIN
All magic is baseless and empty.

མེད་པ་གསལ་སྣང་སྒྱུ་མ་ཆུ་ཟླ་འདྲ། །
MEPA SAL NANG GYUMA CHUDA DRA
Appearing clearly but not existing, like a magic trick or the moon in water.

སྣང་སྟོང་དབྱེར་མེད་དོན་ལ་མཉམ་པར་ཞོག །
NANGTONG YERMÉ DÖN LA NYAMPAR SHOK
Rest in the non-duality of appearance and emptiness, which are equal in reality.

The Flight of Garuda

ད་ལྟ་རང་ཆག་གཉིད་ཀྱི་རྨི་ལམ་ན། །
DA TA RANGCHAK NYI KYI MILAM NA
At present, during sleep, in our dreams,

ཕ་ཡུལ་གནས་ཁང་ཉེ་འབྲེལ་ལ་སོགས་པ། །
PAYUL NÉ KHANG NYEDREL LASOKPA
Our homeland, house, family, friends, and so on,

མངོན་སུམ་སྣང་ནས་བདེ་སྡུག་མྱོང་བའི་ཚེ། །
NGÖNSUM NANG NÉ DEDUK NYONGWÉ TSÉ
Appear vividly to us, and even though we experience happiness and suffering,

རང་གི་ཉེ་དུ་འབྲེལ་པ་གཅིག་ཀྱང་མེད། །
RANG GI NYÉ DU DRELPA CHIK KYANGMÉ
Not even one of our relatives is actually there.

རང་ཉིད་མལ་ནས་ཅུང་ཟད་མ་གཡོས་ཀྱང༌། །
RANGNYI MAL NÉ CHUNGZÉ MA YÖ KYANG
Even though you yourself haven't moved even slightly from your bed,

ཉིན་པར་ཇི་བཞིན་ཉམས་སུ་མངོན་སུམ་མྱོང༌། །
NYINPAR JIZHIN NYAM SU NGÖNSUM NYONG
You directly experience things just like during the day.

དེ་བཞིན་ཚེ་འདིའི་སྣང་བ་ཐམས་ཅད་ཀུན། །
DEZHIN TSÉ DI NANGWA TAMCHÉ KÜN
Likewise, all the appearances of this life,

Song 9 - Magic Projection

མདང་གི་རྨི་ལམ་ཉམས་སུ་མྱོང་པ་བཞིན། །
DANG GI MILAM NYAM SU NYANGPA ZHIN
Are like the experiences of last night's dream.

རང་གི་སེམས་ཀྱིས་དེར་བཏགས་དེར་བཟུང་ནས། །
RANG GI SEM KYI DER TAK DER ZUNG NÉ
Your own mind has labeled and grasped them there,

དེ་ལྟར་སྣང་སྟེ་སེམས་ཀྱི་མྱོང་བ་ཡིན། །
DETAR NANG TÉ SEM KYI NYONGWA YIN
And so they appear and are experienced by the mind.

རྨི་ལམ་གཉིད་ཀྱི་སྐབས་སུ་འང་རང་བཞིན་མེད། །
MILAM NYI KYI KABSU ANG RANGSHIN MÉ
Just as dreams during sleep have no inherent existence,

དེ་བཞིན་ཇི་ལྟར་སྣང་ཡང་སྟོང་པ་འོ།། །།
DEZHIN JITAR NANG YANG TONGPA O
No matter how things appear, they are always empty.

SONG 10

All in the Mind

ཧཱུྃ ཨེ་མ་ཧོ། སྐལ་པར་ལྡན་པའི་སེམས་ཀྱི་བུ་གཅིག་པོ། །
EMAHO KALWAR DENPÉ SEM KYI BU CHIKPO
Emaho! Fortunate, only child of my heart.

སྣང་བ་ཐམས་ཅད་ངེས་པ་མ་ཡིན་ཏེ། །
NANGWA TAMCHÉ NGEPA MAYINTÉ
All appearances are not definite.

ལ་ལས་སྣང་བ་ལ་ལས་མུན་པ་འོ། །
LALÉ NANGWA LALÉ MÜNPA O
For some, there is light, for others, darkness.

དེ་ཡང་སེམས་ཅན་འགའ་ཞིག་ས་གཞི་ལ། །
DÉYANG SEMCHEN GA SHIK SA CHE LA
Furthermore, among sentient beings on earth,

ས་ལ་ས་ཡི་འདུ་ཤེས་སེམས་ཅན་ཡོད། །
SA LA SA YI DÜSHÉ SEMCHEN YÖ
There are sentient beings who perceive earth as earth.

ས་ལ་མེ་ཡི་འདུ་ཤེས་སེམས་ཅན་ཡོད། །
SA LA MÉ YI DÜSHÉ SEMCHEN YÖ
There are sentient beings who perceive earth as fire.

ས་ལ་ལོངས་སྤྱོད་འདུ་ཤེས་སེམས་ཅན་ཡོད། །
SA LA LONGCHÖ DÜSHÉ SEMCHEN YÖ
There are sentient beings who perceive earth as enjoyment.

ས་ལ་སྡུག་བསྔལ་འདུ་ཤེས་སེམས་ཅན་ཡོད། །
SA LA DUKNGAL DÜSHÉ SEMCHEN YÖ
There are sentient beings who perceive earth as suffering.

ཆུ་ལ་ཆུ་ཡི་འདུ་ཤེས་སེམས་ཅན་ཡོད། །
CHU LA CHU YI DÜSHÉ SEMCHEN YÖ
There are sentient beings who perceive water as water.

ཆུ་ལ་མེ་ཡི་འདུ་ཤེས་སེམས་ཅན་ཡོད། །
CHU LA MÉ YI DÜSHÉ SEMCHEN YÖ
There are sentient beings who perceive water as fire.

ཆུ་ལ་བདུད་རྩིར་འདུ་ཤེས་སེམས་ཅན་ཡོད། །
CHU LA DÜTSI DÜSHÉ SEMCHEN YÖ
There are sentient beings who perceive water as nectar.

ཆུ་ལ་གནས་ཁང་འདུ་ཤེས་སེམས་ཅན་ཡོད། །
CHU LA NÉKHANG DÜSHÉ SEMCHEN YÖ
There are sentient beings who perceive water as a home.

ཆུ་ལ་ས་རུ་འདུ་ཤེས་སེམས་ཅན་ཡོད། །
CHU LA SA RU DÜSHÉ SEMCHEN YÖ
There are sentient beings who perceive water as earth.

མེ་ལ་མེ་ཡི་འདུ་ཤེས་སེམས་ཅན་ཡོད། །
MÉ LA MÉ YI DÜSHÉ SEMCHEN YÖ
There are sentient beings who perceive fire as fire.

མེ་ལ་ལོངས་སྤྱོད་འདུ་ཤེས་སེམས་ཅན་ཡོད། །
MÉ LA LONGCHÖ DÜSHÉ SEMCHEN YÖ
There are sentient beings who perceive fire as enjoyment.

མེ་ལ་གནས་སུ་འདུ་ཤེས་སེམས་ཅན་ཡོད། །
MÉ LA NÉ SU DÜSHÉ SEMCHEN YÖ
There are sentient beings who perceive fire as a home.

མེ་ལ་ཟས་སུ་འདུ་ཤེས་སེམས་ཅན་ཡོད། །
MÉ LA ZÉ SU DÜSHÉ SEMCHEN YÖ
There are sentient beings who perceive fire as food.

ནམ་མཁའ་ནམ་མཁར་འདུ་ཤེས་སེམས་ཅན་ཡོད། །
NAMKHA NAMKHAR DÜSHÉ SEMCHEN YÖ
There are sentient beings who perceive space as space.

ནམ་མཁའ་གནས་སུ་འདུ་ཤེས་སེམས་ཅན་ཡོད། །
NAMKHA NÉ SU DÜSHÉ SEMCHEN YÖ
There are sentient beings who perceive space as a home.

ནམ་མཁའ་ས་རུ་འདུ་ཤེས་སེམས་ཅན་ཡོད། །
NAMKHA SA RU DÜSHÉ SEMCHEN YÖ
There are sentient beings who perceive space as earth.

དེས་ན་སྣང་བ་དེས་པ་མེད་པའི་ཕྱིར། །
DENA NANGWA NGEPA MEPÉ CHIR
Therefore, since appearances are not definite,

Song 10 - All in the Mind

བག་ཆགས་དབང་གིས་གང་ལྟར་སྣང་བ་ཡིན། །
BAKCHAK WANG GI GANGTAR NANGWA YIN
However they appear is due to the power of habitual tendencies.

དེ་ལྟར་འབྱུང་བ་བཞི་པོ་རང་རང་དུ། །
DETAR JUNGWA ZHI PO RANGRANG DU
In that way, each of the four elements, individually,

འདུ་ཤེས་པ་ནི་མི་ཡི་སྣང་དོ་ཡིན། །
DÜSHÉ PA NI MI YI NANGNGO YIN
This perception is the appearance of humans.

འགྲོ་བ་གཞན་གྱིས་ས་གཞི་འདི་ལ་ཡང་། །
DROWA SHEN GYI SA ZHI DI LA YANG
Other beings, even on the ground of this earth,

དམྱལ་བའི་མེ་དང་ཞིང་པའི་ལོངས་སྤྱོད་དང་། །
NYALWÉ MÉ DANG ZHINGPÉ LONGCHÖ DANG
Perceive it as the fire of hell, or the farmers fields.

རྒྱུད་ཀྱིས་ནོན་པས་སྡུག་བསྔལ་འདུ་ཤེས་པའོ། །
GYÜ KYI NÖNPÉ DUKNGAL DÜSHÉ PA'O
Or due to being oppressed by karma, they perceive it as suffering.

དེ་བཞིན་མེ་ལ་མེ་ལྷས་ལོངས་སྤྱོད་དང་། །
DEZHIN MÉ LA MÉLHÉ LONGCHÖ DANG
Similarly, in fire — the fire gods perceive enjoyment,

ཡི་དྭགས་མེ་ལུས་ཅན་གྱིས་གནས་ཁང་དང་། །
YI DAK MÉLÜCHEN GYI NÉKHANG DANG
Pretas with fiery bodies perceive a home,

མེ་ཡི་སྲིན་བུས་ཟས་སུ་འདུ་ཤེས་པའོ། །
MÉ YI SINBÜ ZÉ SU DÜSHÉ PA'O
And fire parasites perceive it as food.

དེ་བཞིན་ཆུ་ལ་དམྱལ་བའི་འགྲོ་བས་མེ། །
DEZHIN CHU LA NYALWÉ DROWÉ MÉ
Similarly, in water — hell beings perceive fire,

ཡི་དྭགས་སེམས་ཅན་རྣམས་ལ་རྣག་ཁྲག་དང་། །
YI DAK SEMCHEN NAM LA NAKTHRAK DANG
For pretas, it is pus and blood.

ཧསྟི་གླང་པོས་ས་དང་ལྷས་བདུད་རྩི། །
HASTI LANGPÖ SA DANG LHÉ DÜTSI
Elephants perceive earth, and gods perceive nectar.

གཞན་འཕྲུལ་དབང་བྱེད་ལྷ་ལ་རིན་ཆེན་དང་། །
SHENTHRUL WANGJÉ LHA LA RINCHEN DANG
For the Paranirmitavasavartin gods, it is jewels.

མེ་ཏོག་ཆར་དང་ཀླུ་ཡིས་གནས་ཁང་ངོ་། །
METOK CHAR DANG LÜ YI NÉKHANG NGO
For flowers it is rain, for nagas it is a home.

ནམ་མཁའ་ལ་ཡང་དེ་ལྟར་བྱས་ནས་གནས། །
NAMKHA LA YANG DETAR JÉ NÉ NÉ
The sky also, it is like that.

ལྷ་རྣམས་ཀུན་གྱིས་ས་ཡི་འདུ་ཤེས་སོ། །
LHA NAM KÜN GYI SA YI DÜSHÉ SO
All the gods perceive it as earth.

Song 10 - All in the Mind

དེས་ན་ཐམས་ཅད་རང་གི་གང་ལྟར་དུ། །
DENA TAMCHÉ RANG GI GANGTAR DU
Therefore, everything appears according to how one's own mind perceives it.

བཏགས་པ་དེ་ལྟར་བཞིན་དུ་སྣང་བ་འོ། །
TAKPA DETAR ZHINDU NANGWA O
What is conceptually constructed, appears in just that way.

དེ་ཡང་ལྷ་ཡི་བུ་ཡིས་སངས་རྒྱས་ལ། །
DÉYANG LHA YI BU YI SANGGYÉ LA
Furthermore, a son of the gods asked the Buddha,

རི་རབ་ཉི་ཟླ་ལ་སོགས་སུ་ཡིས་བྱས། །
RI RAB NYIDA LASOK SU YI JÉ
"Who made Mount Meru, the sun, the moon, and so on?"

ཞུས་ཚེ་སངས་རྒྱས་ཉིད་ཀྱི་ཞལ་ནས་ཀྱང་། །
ZHÜ TSÉ SANGGYÉ NYI KYI SHYAL NÉ KYANG
When asked, the Buddha himself said,

འདི་ལ་བྱེད་མཁན་གཞན་ནི་སུ་ཡང་མེད། །
DI LA JÉMKHEN SHEN NI SUYANG MÉ
"There is no other maker of this.

རང་གི་རྟོག་པའི་བག་ཆགས་ཨ་འཐས་ཀྱིས། །
RANG GI TOKPÉ BAKCHAK ATÉ KYI
Due to the concretizing habitual tendencies of one's own thoughts,

དེར་བཏགས་དེར་བཟུང་དེ་ལྟར་སྣང་བ་ཡིན། །
DER TAK DER ZUNG DETAR NANGWA YIN
It is projected there, grasped there, and appears in that way."

The Flight of Garuda

ཐམས་ཅད་རང་གི་སེམས་ཀྱིས་བྱས་པར་གསུངས། །
TAMCHÉ RANG GI SEM KYI JEPAR SUNG
He said that everything is made by one's own mind.

ལྷ་ཡི་བུ་ཡིས་སངས་རྒྱས་ཡང་ཞུས་ཏེ། །
LHA YI BU YI SANGGYÉ YANG ZHÜ TÉ
The son of the gods again asked the Buddha,

རང་གི་རྟོག་པ་ཇི་ལྟར་འཛིན་ཀྱང་། །
RANG GI TOKPA JITAR ATÉ KYANG
"No matter how one clings to one's own concepts,

རི་རབ་ཉི་མ་ཟླ་བ་ལ་སོགས་པའི། །
RI RAB NYIMA DAWA LASOK PÉ
of Mount Meru, the sun and moon, and so on,

སྲ་ཞིང་བརྟན་པ་འདི་འདྲ་ག་ན་འོངས། །
SRA ZHING TENPA DI DRA GA NA ONG
Where did this solid and stable appearance come from?"

ཞུས་ཚེ་སངས་རྒྱས་ཉིད་ཀྱི་ཞལ་ནས་ཀྱང་། །
ZHÜ TSÉ SANGGYÉ NYI KYI SHYAL NÉ KYANG
When asked, the Buddha himself said,

ཝཱ་ར་ཎ་སིར་རྒན་མོས་རང་ལུས་ནི། །
WARANASIR GENMÖ RANG LÜ NI
"In Varanasi, an old woman meditated on her own body as a tiger,

སྟག་ཏུ་བསྒོམས་པས་གྲོང་ཁྱེར་དེ་ཡི་ཀྱང་། །
TAK TU GOM PÉ DRONGKHYER DÉ YI KYANG
Because she meditated so strongly on this, even the people of that city,

Song 10 - All in the Mind

སྡུག་ཏུ་མཐོང་ནས་གྲོང་ཁྱེར་སྟོངས་པས་ན། །
TAK TU TONG NÉ DRONG KHYER TONGPÉ NA
Saw her as a tiger, and the city was emptied.

ཡུན་ནི་ཐུང་དུས་དེ་ལྟར་སྣང་ནུས་ན། །
YÜN NI THUNG NGÜ DETAR NANG NÜ NA
If it could appear like that after only a short time,

སྐྱེ་བ་ཐོག་མ་མེད་ནས་བག་ཆགས་སེམས། །
KYEWA THOKMA MENÉ BAKCHAK SEM
Then the mind with habitual tendencies from beginningless births,

གོམས་ན་འདི་འདྲ་ལོས་སྣང་ཐུབ་པས་གསུངས། །
GOM NA DI DRA LÖ NANG THUBPÉ SUNG
Can certainly appear in this way if it is accustomed to it."

དེས་ན་ཐམས་ཅད་སེམས་ཀྱིས་བྱས་པ་འོ། །
DENA TAMCHÉ SEM KYI JEPA O
Therefore, everything is made by the mind.

དེ་ཡང་ཕྱི་རོལ་མུ་སྟེགས་ཁ་ཅིག་གིས། །
DÉYANG CHIROL MUTEK KHACHIK GI
Furthermore, some non-Buddhists,

འཇིག་རྟེན་འདུ་འཛིའི་གཡེང་བ་འགོག་པའི་ཕྱིར། །
JIKTEN DÜDZI YENGWA GOKPÉ CHIR
In order to stop the distraction of worldly activities,

དབེན་གནས་བསྒོམས་པས་དབེན་གནས་མངོན་སུམ་དུ། །
WEN NÉ GOM PÉ WEN NÉ NGÖNSUM DU
Visualized themselves as being in a solitary place,
through this meditation,

གྲུབ་གནས་གཞན་གྱི་མིས་ཀྱང་མཐོང་བ་བྱུང་། །
DRUB NÉ SHEN GYI MI KYANG TONGWA JUNG
These solitary places were made manifest and even other people saw them.

གཅིག་གིས་ནམ་མཁའ་བྲག་ཏུ་བསྒོམས་ནས་ཀྱང་། །
CHIK GI NAMKHA DRAK TU GOM NÉ KYANG
One person visualized the sky as a rock, through uninterrupted meditation,

བྲག་ཏུ་གྱུར་ནས་ཕུང་པོ་ཐོགས་པ་སྐད། །
DRAK TU GYUR NÉ PHUNGPO THOKPA KÉ
It is said that it truly became a rock and his body was stuck there.

དེས་ན་ཐམས་ཅད་སེམས་ཀྱི་རྟོག་པ་ཡིས། །
DENA TAMCHÉ SEM KYI TOKPA YI
Therefore, everything is made by the mind's conceptual thoughts.

བྱས་པ་ཡིན་པའི་སེམས་ཀྱི་རང་སྣང་སྟེ། །
JÉPA YIN PÉ SEM KYI RANGNANG TÉ
It is the mind's own projection.

རང་སྣང་ཐམས་ཅད་དོན་ལ་སྟོང་པའོ། །
RANGNANG TAMCHÉ DÖN LA TONGPA'O
All these self-projections are ultimately empty.

དེ་ཡང་དམྱལ་བ་ཉི་ཚེའི་སེམས་ཅན་གྱིས། །
DÉYANG NYALWA NYITSÉ SEMCHEN GYI
Furthermore, the short-lived hell beings,

Song 10 - All in the Mind

སྒོ་དང་ཀ་བ་ཐབ་དང་ཐག་པ་སོགས། །
GO DANG KAWA THAB DANG THAKPA SOK
Seeing doors, pillars, stoves, ropes, and so forth,

གཟུགས་སུ་འདུ་ཤེས་སྡུག་བསྔལ་མྱོང་བ་འོ། །
ZUK SU DÜSHÉ DUKNGAL NYONGWA O
Perceive forms of torture and experience suffering.

དེས་ན་སེམས་ཀྱི་རྟོག་པས་གང་ལྟར་དུ། །
DENA SEM KYI TOKPÉ GANGTAR DU
Therefore, however the mind's conceptual thoughts label it,

བཏགས་པ་དེ་ལྟར་བཞིན་དུ་སྣང་བ་འོ། །
TAKPA DETAR ZHINDU NANGWA O
It appears in just that way.

འགྲོ་དྲུག་སེམས་ཀྱི་བདེ་སྡུག་ཐམས་ཅད་ནི། །
DRO DRUK SEM KYI DEDUK TAMCHÉ NI
All the happiness and suffering of the six realms of sentient beings,

རང་གི་སེམས་ཉིད་གཅིག་པུས་བྱས་པའི་ཕྱིར། །
RANG GI SEMNYI CHIKPÜ JEPÉ CHIR
Since it is created by one's own mind alone,

ཐམས་ཅད་རང་གི་སེམས་ཀྱི་ཆོ་འཕྲུལ་གྱིས། །
TAMCHÉ RANG GI SEM KYI CHOTRUL GYI
Everything is the magical display of one's own mind.

མེད་སྣང་སྟོང་པ་ཉིད་ཀྱི་རང་གཟུགས་སུ། །
MÉ NANG TONGPA NYI KYI RANGZUK SU
Recognize it as the very form of emptiness, appearing but not existing.

The Flight of Garuda

བློ་ཐག་ཆོད་ཀྱིས་ཅོད་ལ་ཕྱམ་གྱིས་ཞོག །
LO THAK BÉ KYI CHÖ LA CHAM GYI SHOK
Decide firmly and let it be naturally.

དེ་ཡང་ཐུབ་པ་གངས་ཆེན་མཚོ་ཡི་ནི། །
DÉYANG THUBPA GANGCHEN TSO YI NI
Furthermore, The Buddha 'Infinite Ocean',

ཕྱག་གི་པདྨའི་རྡུལ་གཅིག་སྟེང་ཉིད་ན། །
CHAK GI PEMÉ DUL CHIK TENG NYI NA
On just one dust particle of the lotus in his hand,

སྟོང་གསུམ་མི་མཇེད་འཇིག་རྟེན་ཡོད་པར་གསུངས། །
TONGSUM MIJÉ JIKTEN YÖPAR SUNG
It is said that there exists the three-thousand-fold world system of this Sahā realm.

ཐོད་རྒལ་རིག་པ་ཚད་ལ་ཕེབས་པའི་ཚེ། །
THÖGAL RIGPA TSÉ LA PEBPÉ TSÉ
When Thögal's [9] vision reaches the third state (Vision of Awareness Reaching Fullness)

རང་ལུས་བ་སྤུའི་ཁུང་བུ་རེ་རེ་ན། །
RANG LÜ BASPÜ KHUNG BU RÉ RÉ NA
In each and every pore of one's own body,

---

9. In Dzogchen practice after **Trekchö** (Cutting Through Hardness), there is **Thögal** (Crossing the skull). The main focus of Trekchö is emptiness, the main focus of Thögal is energy appearance, practicing with both light and darkness (Dark retreat).

Song 10 - All in the Mind

སངས་རྒྱས་ཞིང་ཁམས་ཚད་མེད་མཐོང་བ་དང་། །
SANG GYÉ ZHING KHAM TSÉMÉ THONGWA DANG
One sees immeasurable Buddhafields,

འགྲོ་དྲུག་སེམས་ཅན་གནས་ཀྱང་ཚད་མེད་མཐོང་། །
DRO DRUK SEMCHEN NÉ KYANG TSÉMÉ THONG
And one sees immeasurable abodes of the six realms of sentient beings.

དེ་ལ་འགྲོ་འདུལ་སྤྲུལ་པ་བཀྱེ་ནས་ཀྱང་། །
DÉ LA DRODÜL TRULPA KYÉ NÉ KYANG
Within that, by manifesting emanations to tame beings,

རྨི་ལམ་ཇི་བཞིན་འགྲོ་དོན་བྱེད་པར་གསུངས། །
MILAM JIZHIN DRO DÖN JEPAR SUNG
It is said that they perform the benefit of beings just like in a dream.

དེས་ན་འཁོར་འདས་ཆོས་རྣམས་རང་སྣང་ཡིན། །
DENA KHORDÉ CHÖ NAM RANGNANG YIN
Therefore, all phenomena of samsara and nirvana are one's own appearances.

རང་སྣང་ཐམས་ཅད་གཞི་མེད་སྟོང་པ་ཡིན། །
RANGNANG TAMCHÉ SHYIMÉ TONGPA YIN
All one's own appearances are baseless and empty.

སྟོང་གསལ་འཛིན་མེད་ངང་ལ་བློ་གདེང་འཚོས། །
TONGSAL DZINMÉ NGANG LA LO DENG CHÖ
Rest with confidence in the state of empty clarity, without grasping.

The Flight of Garuda

གཞན་ཡང་རྡུལ་གཅིག་སྟེང་ན་རྡུལ་སྙེད་ཀྱི། །
SHEN YANG DUL CHIK TENG NA DUL NYÉ KYI
Furthermore, on one dust particle, there are as many

སངས་རྒྱས་ཞིང་ཁམས་དཔག་ཏུ་མེད་པ་དང་། །
SANGGYÉ ZHING KHAM PAKTU MEPA DANG
Immeasurable Buddhafields as there are dust particles.

འགྲོ་དྲུག་གནས་ཀྱང་གྲངས་མེད་ཡོད་པར་གསུངས། །
DRO DRUK NÉ KYANG DRANGMÉ YÖPAR SUNG
And there are countless abodes of the six realms, it is said.

དེ་རྣམས་ཐམས་ཅད་འདྲེས་མེད་རྙོག་པ་མེད། །
DÉ NAM TAMCHÉ DRÉMÉ NYOKPA MÉ
All of these are unmixed and without confusion.

གནོད་པར་གྱུར་པ་མེད་པར་རྒྱལ་བས་གསུངས། །
NÖPAR GYURPA MEPAR GYALWÉ SUNG
And the Buddha said that they are without harming each other.

གཞན་ཡང་སྲིན་བུ་རེ་རེའི་ཁོག་ན་ཡང་། །
SHEN YANG SINBU RÉ RÉ KHOK NA YANG
Furthermore, even in the belly of each and every insect,

སྲིན་འབུའི་གྲོང་ཁྱེར་དཔག་མེད་ཡོད་པར་གསུངས། །
SINBÜ DRONGKHYER PAKTU MÉ YÖPAR SUNG
It is said that there are immeasurable cities of insects
(micro-organisms)

ནམ་མཁའི་ཁམས་ན་གྲོང་ཁྱེར་མང་པོ་ཡི། །
NAMKHÉ KHAM NA DRONGKHYER MANGPO YI
In the expanse of space, many cities

མགོ་བོ་ཐུར་དུ་བསྟན་ནས་ཆགས་པ་དང་། །
GOWO THUR DU TEN NÉ CHAKPA DANG
are formed with their buildings pointing upside down.

དེ་བཞིན་འཕྲེད་དང་གྱེན་དུ་ཆགས་པ་ཡི། །
DEZHIN THRÉ DANG GYEN DU CHAKPA YI
Similarly, others are formed facing sideways and upwards.

གྲོང་ཁྱེར་དཔག་ཏུ་མེད་པར་ཡོད་པར་གསུངས། །
DRONGKHYER PAKTU MÉPAR YÖPAR SUNG
It is said that there are immeasurable invisible cities.

འདི་འདྲ་འདི་དག་སུ་ཡིས་བྱས་སྙམ་ན། །
DI DRA DI DAK SU YI JÉ NYAM NA
If you think, "Who made all these things?"

ཐམས་ཅད་སེམས་ཀྱིས་བྱས་པར་རྒྱལ་བས་གསུངས། །
TAMCHÉ SEM KYI JEPAR GYALWÉ SUNG
The Buddhas said that everything is made by the mind.

སེམས་ཀྱི་རང་བཞིན་གདོད་ནས་ནམ་མཁའ་འདྲ། །
SEM KYI RANGSHIN DÖNÉ NAMKHA DRA
The nature of mind is primordially like space.

ཆོས་རྣམས་ཐམས་ཅད་དེ་བཞིན་ཤེས་པར་གྱིས། །
CHÖ NAM TAMCHÉ DEZHIN SHÉPAR GYI
Know all phenomena to be like that.

ཀུན་རྫོབ་སྣང་གྲག་ཆོས་རྣམས་ཐམས་ཅད་ཀུན། །
KÜNDZOB NANG DRAK CHÖ NAM TAMCHÉ KÜN
All phenomena of relative appearance and sound,

The Flight of Garuda

རང་གི་སེམས་ཉིད་གཅིག་པུའི་རང་སྣང་སྟེ། །
RANG GI SEMNYI CHIKPÜ RANGNANG TÉ
Are the self-appearance of one's own mind alone.

འཆི་ཚེ་རང་གི་སེམས་རྒྱུད་འགྱུར་བས་ན། །
CHI TSÉ RANG GI SEM GYÜ GYURWÉ NA
At the time of death, one's own mindstream transforms,

ཕྱི་རོལ་འགྱུར་བ་མེད་ཀྱང་རང་སྣང་འགྱུར། །
CHIROL GYURWA MÉ KYANG RANGNANG GYUR
Even if the outer world does not change, one's own experience changes.

དེས་ན་ཐམས་ཅད་སེམས་ཀྱི་རང་སྣང་སྟེ། །
DENA TAMCHÉ SEM KYI RANGNANG TÉ
Therefore, everything is the self-appearance of mind.

རང་སྣང་ཐམས་ཅད་གཞི་མེད་སྟོང་པ་ཡིན། །
RANGNANG TAMCHÉ SHYIMÉ TONGPA YIN
All self-appearances are baseless and empty.

མེད་པ་གསལ་སྣང་གཟུགས་བརྙན་ཆུ་ཟླ་འདྲ། །
MÉPA SAL NANG ZUKNYEN CHUDA DRA
Appearing clearly but not existing, like a reflection of the moon in water.

གསལ་སྟོང་གཉིས་མེད་རིག་པའི་ངང་ཉམས་སྐྱོངས། །
SAL TONG NYIMÉ RIGPÉ NGANG NYAM KYONG
Maintain the practice in the state of clear emptiness, non-dual awareness.

Song 10 - All in the Mind

མཐོང་སྣང་ཐམས་ཅད་སེམས་ཀྱི་རང་སྣང་ཡིན། །
THONGNANG TAMCHÉ SEM KYI RANGNANG YIN
All that is seen is the self-appearance of mind.

སྣོད་ཀྱི་འཇིག་རྟེན་བེམ་པོར་སྣང་བ་སེམས། །
NÖD KYI JIKTEN BEMPOR NANGWA SEM
The appearance of the inanimate environment is mind.

བཅུད་ཀྱི་སེམས་ཅན་རིགས་དྲུག་སྣང་བའང་སེམས། །
CHÜ KYI SEMCHEN RIK DRUK NANG WANG SEM
The appearance of the six realms of sentient beings,
the animate world, is mind as well.

མཐོ་རིས་ལྷ་མིའི་བདེ་བ་སྣང་བའང་སེམས། །
THORI LHAMYI DEWA NANG WANG SEM
The appearance of the happiness of gods and humans
in the higher realms is also mind.

ངན་སོང་གསུམ་གྱི་སྡུག་བསྔལ་སྣང་བའང་སེམས། །
NGENSONG SUM GYI DUKNGAL NANG WANG SEM
The appearance of the suffering of the three lower realms
is mind as well.

མ་རིག་ཉོན་མོངས་དུག་ལྔར་སྣང་བ་སེམས། །
MARIG NYÖNMONG DUK NGAR NANGWA SEM
The appearance of ignorance, afflictions, and the five toxins
is also mind.

རང་བྱུང་ཡེ་ཤེས་རིག་པ་སྣང་བའང་སེམས། །
RANGJUNG YESHE RIGPA NANG WANG SEM
The appearance of self-arising wisdom awareness is mind as well.

དན་རྟོག་འཁོར་བའི་བག་ཆགས་སྣང་བའང་སེམས། །
NGANTOK KHORWÉ BAKCHAK NANG WANG SEM
The appearance of negative thoughts and the habitual tendencies of samsara is also mind.

བཟང་རྟོག་སངས་རྒྱས་ཞིང་ཁམས་སྣང་བའང་སེམས། །
ZANGTOK SANGGYÉ ZHINGKHAM NANG WANG SEM
The appearance of good thoughts and Buddhafields is mind as well.

བདུད་དང་འདྲེ་ཡིས་བར་ཆད་སྣང་བའང་སེམས། །
DÜD DANG DRÉ YI BARCHÉ NANG WANG SEM
The appearance of obstacles from demons and spirits is also mind.

ལྷ་དང་དངོས་གྲུབ་ལེགས་པར་སྣང་བའང་སེམས། །
LHA DANG NGÖDRUB LEKPAR NANG WANG SEM
The appearance of deities and spiritual accomplishments is mind as well.

རྣམ་པར་རྟོག་པ་སྣ་ཚོགས་སྣང་བའང་སེམས། །
NAMPAR TOKPA NATSOK NANG WANG SEM
The appearance of various conceptual thoughts is also mind.

མི་རྟོག་རྩེ་གཅིག་སྒོམ་པར་སྣང་བའང་སེམས། །
MITOK TSÉCHIK GOMPAR NANG WANG SEM
The appearance of meditating single-pointedly without thought is mind as well.

དངོས་པོ་མཚན་མ་ཁ་དོག་སྣང་བའང་སེམས། །
NGÖPO TSHENMA KHADOK NANG WANG SEM
The appearance of tangible things, signs, and colors is also mind.

Song 10 - All in the Mind

མཚན་མ་མེད་ཅིང་སྤྲོས་པ་མེད་པའང་སེམས། །
TSHENMA MÉ CHING TRÖPA MÉ PANG SEM
The appearance of being without characteristics and complexity is mind as well.

གཅིག་དང་དུ་མ་གཉིས་མེད་སྣང་བའང་སེམས། །
CHIK DANG DUMA NYIMÉ NANG WANG SEM
The appearance of one, many, and non-duality is also mind.

ཡོད་མེད་གང་ཡང་མ་གྲུབ་སྣང་བའང་སེམས། །
YÖMÉ GANGYANG MADRUB NANG WANG SEM
The appearance of nothing whatsoever being established as existent or non-existent is mind as well.

སེམས་ལས་མ་གཏོགས་སྣང་བ་གང་ཡང་མེད། །
SEM LÉ MATOK NANGWA GANGYANG MÉ
There is no appearance whatsoever apart from mind.

སེམས་ནི་དཔེར་ན་རི་མོ་མཁན་དང་འདྲ། །
SEM NI PER NA RIMO KHEN DANG DRA
Mind is like a painter.

རང་གི་ལུས་ཀྱང་སེམས་ཀྱིས་བྱས་པ་སྟེ། །
RANG GI LÜ KYANG SEM KYI JEPA TÉ
Even one's own body is shaped by the mind.

སྟོང་གསུམ་འཇིག་རྟེན་ཁམས་ནི་ཇི་སྙེད་པ། །
TONGSUM JIKTEN KHAM NI JISNYÉPA
However many thousand million world systems there are,

དེ་དག་ཐམས་ཅད་སེམས་ཀྱི་བྲིས་པ་སྟེ། །
DÉ DAK TAMCHÉ SEM KYI DRIPATÉ
All of them are painted by the mind.

རང་གི་རྟོག་པས་བྲིས་པའི་རི་མོ་ཡིས། །
RANG GI TOKPÉ DRIPÉ RIMO YI
By the paintings drawn by one's own conceptual thoughts,

བྱིས་པའི་བློ་ཅན་འགྲོ་ཀུན་བསླུས་པ་ཡིན། །
JIPÉ LO CHEN DRO KÜN LÜPÉ YIN
All beings with childish minds are cheated.

དེས་ན་ཐམས་ཅད་སེམས་ཀྱི་ཆོ་འཕྲུལ་དུ། །
DENA TAMCHÉ SEM KYI CHOTRUL DU
Therefore, everything is the magic of the mind,

ཐག་ཆོད་ངེས་ཤེས་བསྐྱེད་པ་གལ་ཆེ་འོ། །
THAK CHÖ NGÉ SHÉ KYEPA GAL CHÉ O
To develop a deep understanding of this is very important.

འདི་ནི་རྣམ་རྟོག་སེམས་སུ་དོ་སྟོན་དོ།། །།
DI NI NAMTOK SEM SU NGÖTRO DO
This is the introduction to conceptual thoughts as mind.

SONG 11

Emptiness, Appearance, Awareness

ཧོ༔ ཨེ་མ་ཧོ། ད་ཡང་སེམས་ཀྱི་བུ་མཆོག་ཐམས་ཅད་ཉོན། །
EMAHO DA YANG SEM KYI BU CHOK TAMCHÉ NYÖN
Emaho! Now again, listen, all supreme sons and daughters of my heart!

དེ་ལྟར་བྱེད་མཁན་རང་གི་སེམས་ཉིད་ལ། །
DETAR JÉMKHEN RANG GI SEMNYI LA
Look at your own mind, the one that does all this.

ངོ་བོ་ངོས་གཟུང་དབྱིབས་དང་ཁ་དོག་སོགས། །
NGOWO NGÖZUNG YIB DANG KHADOK SOK
Its essence, how to identify it, its shape, color, and so on,

སངས་རྒྱས་ཀྱིས་ཀྱང་བསྟན་དུ་མེད་པ་སྟེ། །
SANGGYÉ KYI KYANG TENDU MEPA TÉ
Even the Buddha can't point it out.

ཡེ་ནས་སྟོང་པ་འཛིན་མེད་ནམ་མཁའ་འདྲ། །
YENÉ TONGPA DZINMÉ NAMKHA DRA
It is primordially empty, without grasping, like the sky.

The Flight of Garuda

སེམས་ཉིད་སྟོང་པ་གཞི་མེད་ཡིན་པར་ངེས། །
SEMNYI TONGPA SHYIMÉ YINPAR NGÉ
Know with certainty that mind itself is empty and without a basis.

སེམས་ཉིད་མཚོན་དོན་ནམ་མཁའ་དཔེར་བཞག་ཀྱང་། །
SEMNYI TSÖN DÖN NAMKHA PER SHYAK KYANG
Even though the sky is given as an example to represent mind,

རེ་ཞིག་སྟོང་ཕྱོགས་ཙམ་གྱི་མཚོན་དཔེའི་སྟེ། །
RÉ SHYIK TONG CHOK TSAM GYI TSÖNPÉ TÉ
It is only a temporary example to represent the aspect of emptiness.

སེམས་ཉིད་རིག་བཅས་སྟོང་པ་ཅིར་ཡང་འཆར། །
SEMNYI RIKCHÉ TONGPA CHIRYANG CHAR
Mind's nature is both empty and aware, and anything can arise in it.

ནམ་མཁའ་རིག་མེད་སྟོང་ཆད་ཧ་པོ་སྟེ། །
NAMKHA RIKMÉ TONGCHÉ HAPO TÉ
The sky is empty, but without awareness, a blank nothingness,

དེའི་ཕྱིར་སེམས་དོན་ནམ་མཁས་མཚོན་དུ་མེད། །
DÉ CHIR SEM DÖN NAMKHÉ TSÖN DU MÉ
Therefore, the meaning of mind cannot be represented by the sky.

འདི་ནི་སེམས་ཉིད་སྟོང་པར་ངོ་སྤྲོད་དོ། །
DI NI SEMNYI TONGPAR NGÖTRO DO
This is the introduction to the emptiness of mind itself.

སེམས་ཉིད་གསལ་སྟོང་དེ་ཡི་རང་རྩལ་ལས། །
SEMNYI SALS TONG DÉ YI RANG TZAL LÉ
From the inherent power of mind itself, which is clear and empty.

Song 11 - Emptiness, Appearance, Awareness

སྣང་བ་སྣ་ཚོགས་གང་ཡང་འཆར་བ་ཡིན། །
NANGWA NATSOK GANGYANG CHARWA YIN
Any kind of various appearances arise.

ཤར་ཡང་མེ་ལོང་ནང་གི་གཟུགས་བརྙན་བཞིན། །
SHAR YANG MELONG NANG GI ZUKNYEN ZHIN
As they arise, they are like reflections in a mirror.

གཉིས་སུ་མེད་དེ་སྟོང་པའི་ངང་དུ་གཅིག །
NYISU MÉ DÉ TONGPÉ NGANG DU CHIK
They are non-dual, one within the state of emptiness.

འདི་ནི་སྟོང་པ་སྣང་བར་ངོ་སྤྲོད་དོ། །
DI NI TONGPA NANGWAR NGÖTRO DO
This is the introduction to emptiness as appearances.

ཡེ་ནས་སྣང་སྟོང་གཉིས་སུ་མེད་པ་སྟེ། །
YENÉ NANGTONG NYISU MEPA TÉ
Primordially, appearance and emptiness are non-dual.

རང་སེམས་སྟོང་པས་སྣང་བ་མི་འགག་ཅིང་། །
RANGSEM TONGPÉ NANGWA MI GAK CHING
Because your own mind is empty, appearances do not cease.

སྟོང་པའི་ངང་ལས་སྣང་བ་འཛིན་མེད་བཀྲ། །
TONGPÉ NGANG LÉ NANGWA DZINMÉ TRA
From the state of emptiness, appearances shine without grasping.

སྣང་བ་རྣམས་ཀྱིས་སྟོང་པ་མི་འགག་ཅིང་། །
NANGWA NAM KYI TONGPA MI GAK CHING
Because of appearances, emptiness does not cease.

སྣང་ཡང་རང་བཞིན་ཡེ་ནས་སྟོང་པ་འོ། །
NANG YANG RANGSHIN YENÉ TONGPA O
Though appearing, its nature is primordially empty.

ནམ་མཁའི་འཇའ་ཚོན་ཆུ་ནང་ཟླ་གཟུགས་ལྟར། །
NAMKHÉ JATSÖN CHU NANG DA ZUK TAR
Like a rainbow in the sky or a reflection of the moon in water,

སྣང་སྟོང་གཉིས་མེད་རྟོགས་པའི་རྣལ་འབྱོར་ལ། །
NANGTONG NYIMÉ TOKPÉ NALJOR LA
For a yogi who has realized the non-duality of appearance-emptiness,

འཁོར་འདས་ཆོས་རྣམས་སྒྱུ་མའི་ལྟད་མོ་ཡིན། །
KHORDÉ CHÖ NAM GYUMÉ TADMO YIN
All phenomena of samsara and nirvana are like a magical show.

སྣང་སྟོང་གཉིས་མེད་ལྟད་མོར་བལྟས་པའི་ཚེ། །
NANGTONG NYIMÉ TADMOR TÉPÉ TSÉ
When looking at the show of non-dual appearance-emptiness,

བློ་སེམས་འགྱུར་བ་མེད་པའི་རྣལ་འབྱོར་བདེ། །
LO SEM GYURWA MEPÉ NALJOR DÉ
There is the bliss of a yogi whose mind does not waver.

དེ་ལྟར་ཡིན་མིན་སྐལ་ལྡན་བུ་རྣམས་ཀུན། །
DETAR YIN MIN KALDEN BU NAM KÜN
To know whether it is like that or not, all fortunate ones,

རང་སེམས་སྟོང་པ་ཉིད་དང་སྣང་བ་གཉིས། །
RANGSEM TONGPA NYI DANG NANGWA NYI
Your own mind, its emptiness and its appearances,

Song 11 - Emptiness, Appearance, Awareness

སོ་སོར་དབྱེ་རྒྱུ་ཨེ་ཡོད་བལྟོས་དང་ཤེས། །
SOSOR YÉ GYU É YÖ TÖ DANG SHÉ
Look and see if there is any way to separate them.

ཡེ་ནས་སྣང་སྟོང་གཉིས་སུ་མེད་པ་འོ། །
YENÉ NANGTONG NYISU MEPA O
Pervasively, appearance and emptiness are non-dual.

འདི་ནི་སྣང་སྟོང་གཉིས་མེད་རོ་སྟོད་དོ། །
DI NI NANGTONG NYIMÉ NGÖTRO DO
This is the introduction to the non-duality
of appearance-emptiness.

དེ་ལྟར་སྣང་སྟོང་གཉིས་མེད་རང་བྱུང་གི །
DETAR NANGTONG NYIMÉ RANGJUNG GI
In that way, naturally arising undivided appearance-emptiness,

རིག་པ་རང་གསལ་ས་ལེ་ཧྲིག་གེ་བ། །
RIGPA RANGSAL SALÉ HRIK GÉ WA
This self-clear, vivid, and bright awareness,

སྐུ་གསུམ་ལྷུན་གྱིས་གྲུབ་པའི་དགོངས་པ་སྟེ། །
KU SUM LHÜN GYI DRUBPÉ GONGPA TÉ
Is the realization where the three kayas are spontaneously accomplished.

ཐུན་མཚམས་མེད་པར་འཁོར་ཡུག་ཉམས་ལེན་ལ། །
THÜNTSAM MEPAR KHORYUK NYAMLEN LA
Practice continuously wherever you are.

The Flight of Garuda

ཉིན་མཚན་མེད་པར་སྐྱོངས་ཤིག་སེམས་ཀྱི་བུ། །
NYIN TSHEN MEPAR KYONG SHYIK SEM KYI BU
Maintain it day and night, children of my heart.

འདི་ནི་གཉིས་མེད་རང་གྲོལ་དོ་སྟོད་དོ།། །།
DI NI NYIMÉ RANGDROL NGÖTRO DO
This is the introduction to non-dual self-liberation.

SONG 12

Recognizing the Ground's Three Kayas

ཧྰུྃ ཨེ་མ་ཧོ། ད་ཡང་བྱ་བཏང་བདག་གི་གླུ་ལ་ཉོན། །
EMAHO DA YANG JATANG DAK GI LU LA NYÖN
Emaho! Now again, listen to the song of this wandering renunciate.

གཞི་ཡི་རིག་པར་སྐུ་གསུམ་ཚང་ཚུལ་དང་། །
ZHI YI RIGPA KU SUM TSANG TSUL DANG
The way the three kayas are complete within the ground's awareness,

གཞི་སྣང་དུས་ཀྱི་སྐུ་གསུམ་ཚང་ཚུལ་གྱི། །
ZHI NANG DÜ KYI KU SUM TSANG TSUL GYI
And the way the three kayas are complete at the time of the ground's appearance,

རྣམ་དབྱེ་འདི་གཉིས་ལེགས་པར་ཤེས་བྱས་ནས། །
NAM DYÉ DI NYI LEKPAR SHÉ JÉ NÉ
Clearly understanding these two distinctions,

འཁོར་འདས་སྐུ་གསུམ་ཞིང་དུ་རྟོགས་པར་བྱ། །
KHORDÉ KU SUM ZHING DU TOKPAR JA
You will recognize samsara and nirvana as the very realm of the three kayas.

The Flight of Garuda

གཞི་ཡི་རིག་པར་སྐུ་གསུམ་ཚང་ཚུལ་ནི། །
ZHI YI RIGPAR KU SUM TSANG TSUL NI
The way the three kayas are complete in the ground awareness is:

སྔོན་དུའང་བཤད་ཀྱང་ད་དུང་འདིར་ཡང་འཆད། །
NGÖN DU'ANG SHÉ KYANG DADUNG DIR YANG CHÉ
Although explained before, I will explain it again here.

རང་རིག་གཞི་ནི་ཤེལ་གྱི་གོང་བུ་འདྲ། །
RANGRIK ZHI NI SHEL GYI GONGBU DRA
The ground of self-awareness is like a crystal ball.

དེ་ཡི་སྟོང་པ་ཆོས་སྐུའི་རང་བཞིན་དང་། །
DÉ YI TONGPA CHÖ KÜ RANGSHIN DANG
Its emptiness is the nature of Dharmakaya.

གསལ་བའི་རང་གདངས་ལོངས་སྤྱོད་རྫོགས་པ་དང་། །
SALWÉ RANG DANG LONGCHÖ DZOKPA DANG
Its clear, inherent radiance is Sambhogakaya.

འཆར་གཞི་མ་འགགས་སྒོ་ནི་སྤྲུལ་པའི་སྐུ། །
CHARZHI MA GAK GO NI TRULPÉ KU
Its unceasing display is Nirmanakaya.

གཞི་ཡི་རིག་པར་སྐུ་གསུམ་ཚང་ཚུལ་ཡིན། །
ZHI YI RIGPAR KU SUM TSANG TSUL YIN
This is how the three kayas are complete within ground awareness.

འདི་ལ་ནམ་ཡང་འདུ་འབྲལ་མེད་པ་འོ། །
DI LA NAMYANG DUDRAL MEPA O
In this, there is never any coming together or separation.

Song 12 - Recognizing the Ground's Three Kayas

དཔེར་ན་ཤེལ་ལས་འོད་ལྔ་འཆར་བ་བཞིན། །
PER NA SHEL LÉ Ö NGA SHARWA ZHIN
For example, like five colors of rainbow light arising from a crystal,

དེ་ལས་འཆར་བ་གཞི་སྣང་དུས་ན་ཡང་། །
DÉ LÉ SHARWA ZHI NANG DÜ NA YANG
All the ground's appearances arise in the same manner.

དག་པ་རྒྱལ་བའི་ཞིང་ཁམས་སྣང་བ་དང་། །
DAKPA GYALWÉ ZHINGKHAM NANGWA DANG
Whether it is the appearance of pure Buddhafields,

མ་དག་སྣོད་བཅུད་སྣང་བ་གང་སྣང་ཡང་། །
MADAK NÖ CHÜ NANGWA GANG NANG YANG
Or any appearance of impure environments and beings,

ཐམས་ཅད་ངོ་བོ་སྟོང་པ་ཆོས་ཀྱི་སྐུ། །
TAMCHÉ NGOWO TONGPA CHÖ KYI KU
The essence of all is empty Dharmakaya.

རང་བཞིན་སྣང་བ་ལོངས་སྤྱོད་རྫོགས་པའི་སྐུ། །
RANGSHIN NANGWA LONGCHÖ DZOKPÉ KU
Its (nature) inherent appearance is Sambhogakaya.

སྣ་ཚོགས་མ་འགགས་འཆར་བ་སྤྲུལ་པའི་སྐུ། །
NATSOK MA GAK SHARWA TRULPÉ KU
Its diverse, unceasing manifestation (compassion) is Nirmanakaya.

གཞི་སྣང་དུས་ཀྱི་སྐུ་གསུམ་ཚང་ཚུལ་ལོ། །
ZHI NANG DÜ KYI KU SUM TSANG TSUL LO
This is how the three kayas are complete at the time of the grounds appearance.

གཞན་དུ་འདི་ཡི་རྣམ་དབྱེ་བྱེ་བ་ཉུང་། །
SHENDU DI YI NAMDYÉ CHYEWA NYUNG
Elsewhere, explanations of this distinction are rare.

གནད་འདི་ལེགས་པར་རྟོགས་དགོས་པ་ཞིག་ཡིན། །
NED DI LEKPAR TOK GÖPA SHYIK YIN
This key point is something that needs to be well understood.

ངས་ཀྱང་ཀུན་མཁྱེན་ལེགས་བཤད་དྲིན་ལས་ཤེས། །
NGÉ KYANG KÜNKHYEN LEKSHÉ DRINLÉ SHÉ
I know this through the kindness of the excellent explanations of Omniscient Longchenpa.

དེ་ལྟར་ཤེས་ན་སྣང་སྲིད་ཐམས་ཅད་ཀྱང་། །
DETAR SHÉ NA NANGSI TAMCHÉ KYANG
If you understand in that way, all of appearance and existence,

སྐུ་གསུམ་ལྷུན་གྲུབ་དཀྱིལ་འཁོར་ཡེ་ནས་ཡིན། །
KU SUM LHÜNDRUB KYILKHOR YENÉ YIN
Are primordially the spontaneously accomplished mandala of the three kayas.

སྐུ་གསུམ་ཞིང་ཁམས་གཞན་ནས་བཙལ་དུ་མེད། །
KU SUM ZHINGKHAM SHEN NÉ TSAL DU MÉ
The realm of the three kayas is not to be sought elsewhere.

Song 12 - Recognizing the Ground's Three Kayas

འགྲོ་དྲུག་སེམས་ཅན་རྣམས་ཀྱང་སྐུ་གསུམ་དུ། །
DRO DRUK SEMCHEN NAM KYANG KU SUM DU
The sentient beings of the six realms are also in the three kayas,

གནས་པ་ཡིན་ཏེ་རང་ངོ་ཤེས་ནུས་ན། །
NÉPA YINTÉ RANG NGO SHÉ NÜ NA
It is the abiding state. If they recognize their own nature,

འགྲོ་བ་རྣམས་ཀྱིས་སྒོམ་པ་དུལ་ཙམ་ཡང་། །
DROWA NAM KYI GOMPA DUL TSAM YANG
Then beings would not need to do even a speck of meditation.

བྱ་མི་དགོས་པར་ཐམས་ཅད་འཚང་རྒྱ་འོ། །
JA MI GÖPAR TAMCHÉ TSANG GYA O
Without needing to do anything, all would become awakened.

དེ་ཡང་དོན་ལ་གཞི་ཡི་སྐུ་གསུམ་ཡང་། །
DÉYANG DÖN LA ZHI YI KU SUM YANG
Furthermore, in reality, those three kayas of the ground,

ཆོས་སྐུ་ཡིན་པས་སོ་སོར་མ་འཛིན་ཅིག །
CHÖ KU YIN PÉ SOSOR MA DZIN CHIK
Since they are Dharmakaya, do not grasp at them as separate.

གཞི་སྣང་དུས་ཀྱི་སྐུ་གསུམ་དེ་ཉིད་ཀྱང་། །
ZHI NANG DÜ KYI KU SUM DÉ NYI KYANG
Those three kayas of the ground's appearance,

གཟུགས་སྐུ་ཡིན་པས་སོ་སོར་མ་འཛིན་ཅིག །
ZUK KU YIN PÉ SOSOR MA DZIN CHIK
Since they are Rupakaya (appearance body), do not grasp them as separate.

ཆོས་གཟུགས་གཉིས་ཀྱང་དོན་ལ་སོ་སོར་མིན། །
CHÖ ZUK NYI KYANG DÖN LA SOSOR MIN
Even the two, Dharmakaya and Rupakaya, are not separate in reality;

སྟོང་པ་ཆོས་སྐུའི་ངང་དུ་རོ་གཅིག་གོ །
TONGPA CHÖ KÜ NGANG DU RO CHIK GO
They are of one taste in the state of empty Dharmakaya.

མཐར་ཐུག་གཞི་སྣང་གཞི་ལ་རང་ཐིམ་ནས། །
THARTHUK ZHI NANG ZHI LA RANG THIM NÉ
Ultimately, when the ground's appearance dissolves back into the ground,

གཞི་ཡི་ཆོས་སྐུའི་དགོངས་པ་མངོན་གྱུར་ཚེ། །
ZHI YI CHÖ KÜ GONGPA NGÖN GYUR TSÉ
And realization of the Dharmakaya of the ground becomes obvious,

དོན་གྱི་འབྲས་བུ་མངོན་དུ་གྱུར་པ་ཡིན། །
DÖN GYI DREBU NGÖN DU GYURPA YIN
The ultimate result will have become manifest.

དེ་ནས་ཆོས་སྐུའི་མཁའ་ལས་མ་གཡོས་བཞིན། །
DÉ NÉ CHÖ KÜ KHA LÉ MA YÖ ZHIN
Then, without moving from the sky of Dharmakaya.

Song 12 - Recognizing the Ground's Three Kayas

གཟུགས་སྐུ་རྣམ་གཉིས་འཇའ་ཚོན་ཇི་བཞིན་དུ། །
ZUK KU NAM NYI JATSÖN JI ZHIN DU
The two Rupakayas [10], like a rainbow,

བསྟན་ནས་འགྲོ་དོན་རྒྱུན་མི་འཆད་པ་འོ།། །།
TEN NÉ DRO DÖN GYÜN MI CHÉPA O
Will appear and benefit beings continuously.

---

10. Nirmanakaya & Sambhogakaya

SONG 13

Self Liberation of Five Toxins

༄༅། ཨེ་མ་ཧོ། ད་ཡང་བྱ་བཏང་བདག་གི་གླུ་ལ་ཉོན། །
EMAHO DA YANG JATANG DAK GI LU LA NYÖN
Emaho! Now again, listen to the song of this renunciate.

ཁྱེད་རང་རྣམས་ལ་སྔོན་ལ་གནོད་པ་བསྐྱལ། །
KHYERANG NAM LA NGÖN LA NÖPA KYAL
Think about how you were traumatized by others.

སུན་ནི་དབྱུང་དང་བརྡུང་བཙོག་བྱས་པ་དང་། །
SÜN NI YUNG DANG DRUNG TSOK JEPA DANG
How they have bullied you, beaten you, and treated you badly.

ངོ་ཚ་གཏད་དང་སེམས་ལ་གནོད་པའི་ལས། །
NGOTSA TÉ DANG SEM LA NÖPÉ LÉ
How they have made you ashamed and made you feel guilt and pain.

ཇི་ལྟར་གཞན་གྱིས་བྱས་པའི་ཚུལ་རྣམས་ཀུན། །
JITAR SHEN GYI JEPÉ TSUL NAM KÜN
Think carefully about all the ways others have treated you.

Song 13 - Self Liberation of Five Toxins

རང་གི་ཡིད་ལ་ཚུལ་བཞིན་བསམ་བྱས་ནས། །
RANG GI YI LA TSULZHIN SAM JÉ NÉ
Dive deeply in your mind, and properly reflect.

ཞེ་སྡང་སྐྱེར་ཆུག་སྐྱེས་ཚེ་དོ་བོ་ལ། །
SHÉDANG KYERCHUK KYÉ TSÉ NGOWO LA
Let anger (rage) arise, look directly at its essence.

ཅེར་གྱིས་ལྟོས་ལ་ཞེ་སྡང་མཁན་པོ་དེ། །
CHER GYI TÖ LA SHÉDANG KHENPO DÉ
Look intently at that anger projector.

དང་པོ་གང་ནས་བྱུང་དང་ད་ལྟའི་དུས། །
DANGPO GANG NÉ JUNG DANG DA TI DÜ
Where did it come from in the beginning?

གང་དུ་གནས་དང་ཐ་མ་གང་དུ་འགྲོ། །
GANG DU NÉ DANG THAMA GANG DU DRO
Where does it abide now? And where will it go in the end?

དབྱིབས་དང་ཁ་དོག་ལ་སོགས་ཨེ་འདུག་ལྟོས། །
YIB DANG KHADOK LASOK É DUK TÖ
Look to see if it has a shape, color, etc.

བལྟས་ཚེ་ཡེ་ནས་སྟོང་པ་འཛིན་མེད་ཡིན། །
TÉ TSÉ YENÉ TONGPA DZINMÉ YIN
When you look, it is primordially empty and without grasping.

ཞེ་སྡང་མ་སྤངས་མེ་ལོང་ཡེ་ཤེས་སོ། །
SHÉDANG MAPANG MELONG YESHE SO
Without denying anger, it's liberated as mirror-like wisdom.

ཁྱེད་རྣམས་སྙིང་ལ་སྡུག་པའི་བུད་མེད་དང་། །
KHYERANG NYING LA DUKPÉ BÜMÉ DANG
Now, think about an attractive man or woman,

ཤ་སོགས་རང་ཉིད་ཟ་མ་གང་འདོད་དང་། །
SHA SOK RANGNYI ZAMA GANG DÖ DANG
Or whatever food you desire to eat
(such as sugar, chocolate, meat, etc.)

གོས་སོགས་རང་གི་གོན་པ་གང་འདོད་དང་། །
GÖ SOK RANG GI GÖNPA GANG DÖ DANG
Or whatever clothes you desire to wear.

རྟ་སོགས་རང་གི་ཕྱུགས་རྣམས་གང་འདོད་རྣམས། །
TA SOK RANG GI CHUK NAM GANG DÖ NAM
Or whatever animals, like horses, you yourself desire [11].

ཚུལ་བཞིན་རང་གི་ཡིད་ལ་བསམ་བྱས་ནས། །
TSULZHIN RANG GI YI LA SAM JÉ NÉ
Thinking properly about them in your own mind,

འདོད་ཆགས་སྐྱེར་ཆུག་སྐྱེས་ཚེ་ངོ་བོ་ལ། །
DÖCHAK KYERCHUK KYÉ TSÉ NGOWO LA
When strong desire arises, look directly at its essence.

ཅེར་གྱིས་བལྟོས་ལ་འདོད་ཆགས་མཁན་པོ་དེ། །
CHER GYI TÖ LA DÖCHAK KHENPO DÉ
Look intently at that desire projector.

---

[11]. Modern day: cars, houses, land, money, etc.

Song 13 - Self Liberation of Five Toxins

དང་པོ་གང་ནས་བྱུང་དང་ད་ལྟའི་དུས། །
DANGPO GANG NÉ JUNG DANG DA TI DÜ
Where did it come from in the beginning?

གང་དུ་གནས་དང་ཐ་མ་གང་དུ་འགྲོ། །
GANG DU NÉ DANG THAMA GANG DU DRO
Where does it abide now? And where will it go in the end?

དབྱིབས་དང་ཁ་དོག་ལ་སོགས་ཨེ་འདུག་ལྟོས། །
YIB DANG KHADOK LASOK É DUK TÖ
Look to see if it has a shape, color, etc.

བལྟས་ཚེ་ཡེ་ནས་སྟོང་པ་འཛིན་མེད་ཡིན། །
TÉ TSÉ YENÉ TONGPA DZINMÉ YIN
When you look, it is primordially empty and without grasping.

འདོད་ཆགས་མ་སྤངས་སོར་རྟོག་ཡེ་ཤེས་སོ། །
DÖCHAK MAPANG SORTOK YESHE SO
Without denying desire, it is liberated as discriminating wisdom.

ཁྱེད་རྣམས་གཉིད་དང་བྱིང་རྨུགས་ལ་སོགས་པའི། །
KHYERANG NYI DANG JING MUK LASOK PÉ
Think about strong dullness like sleepiness and drowsiness.

གཏི་མུག་སྐྱེར་ཆུག་སྐྱེས་ཚེ་ངོ་བོ་ལ། །
TIMUK KYERCHUK KYÉ TSÉ NGOWO LA
When ignorance arises, look directly at its essence.

ཅེར་གྱིས་ལྟོས་ལ་གཏི་མུག་མཁན་པོ་དེ། །
CHER GYI TÖ LA TIMUK KHENPO DÉ
Look intently at the projector of ignorance.

དང་པོ་གང་ནས་བྱུང་དང་ད་ལྟའི་དུས། །
DANGPO GANG NÉ JUNG DANG DA TI DÜ
Where did it come from in the beginning?

གང་དུ་གནས་དང་ཐ་མ་གང་དུ་འགྲོ། །
GANG DU NÉ DANG THAMA GANG DU DRO
Where does it abide now? And where will it go in the end?

དབྱིབས་དང་ཁ་དོག་ལ་སོགས་ཨེ་འདུག་ལྟོས། །
YIB DANG KHADOK LASOK É DUK TÖ
Look to see if it has a shape, color, etc.

བལྟས་ཚེ་ཡེ་ནས་སྟོང་པ་འཛིན་མེད་ཡིན། །
TÉ TSÉ YENÉ TONGPA DZINMÉ YIN
When you look, it is primordially empty and without grasping.

གཏི་མུག་མ་སྤངས་ཆོས་དབྱིངས་ཡེ་ཤེས་སོ། །
TIMUK MAPANG CHÖYING YESHE SO
Without denying ignorance, it is liberated as the wisdom of the expanse of reality (Dharmadhātu).

ཁྱེད་རྣམས་རང་གི་རིགས་རུས་སྟོབས་འབྱོར་དང་། །
KHYERANG RANG GI RIK RÜ TOBJOR DANG
Think about your own family lineage, wealth, and power (social status),

གཟུགས་བྱད་ལེགས་དང་ངག་གི་དབྱངས་སྙན་དང་། །
ZUKJYÉ LEK DANG NGAK GI YANG NYEN DANG
Your good looks and good voice (body image and facial beauty),

Song 13 - Self Liberation of Five Toxins

ཐོས་བསམ་སྒོམ་གསུམ་ཡི་གེ་འབྲི་ཀློག་དང་། །
THÖ SAM GOM SUM YIGÉ DRI LOK DANG
Your learning, contemplation, meditation, writing, and reading,

རིག་གནས་མཁས་དང་གྲོང་ཆོག་གདུལ་བྱ་སོགས། །
RIGNÉ KHÉ DANG DRONGCHOK DÜLJA SOK
Your skill in arts and sciences, your ability to guide disciples in rituals, etc.

རང་ལ་ཡོད་ཚད་ཡོན་ཏན་བསམ་བྱས་ནས། །
RANG LA YÖ TSÉ YÖNTEN SAM JÉ NÉ
Thinking about all the good qualities you possess,

གཞན་ལས་ཅུང་ཟད་ང་བཟང་སྙམ་པ་ཡི། །
SHEN LÉ CHUNGZÉ NGA ZANG NYAMPA YI
The thought arises that, "I am a little better than others."

ང་རྒྱལ་སྐྱེར་ཆུག་སྐྱེས་ཚེ་ངོ་བོ་ལ། །
NGAGYAL KYERCHUK KYÉ TSÉ NGOWO LA
When pride arises, look directly at its essence.

ཅེར་གྱིས་ལྟོས་ལ་ང་རྒྱལ་མཁན་པོ་དེ། །
CHER GYI TÖ LA NGAGYAL KHENPO DÉ
Look intently at the projector of pride.

དང་པོ་གང་ནས་བྱུང་དང་ད་ལྟའི་དུས། །
DANGPO GANG NÉ JUNG DANG DA TI DÜ
Where did it come from in the beginning?

གང་དུ་གནས་དང་ཐ་མ་གང་དུ་འགྲོ། །
GANG DU NÉ DANG THAMA GANG DU DRO
Where does it abide now? And where will it go in the end?

དབྱིབས་དང་ཁ་དོག་ལ་སོགས་ཨེ་འདུག་ལྟོས། །
YIB DANG KHADOK LASOK É DUK TÖ
Look to see if it has a shape, color, etc.

བལྟས་ཚེ་ཡེ་ནས་སྟོང་པ་འཛིན་མེད་ཡིན། །
TÉ TSÉ YENÉ TONGPA DZINMÉ YIN
When you look, it is primordially empty and without grasping.

ང་རྒྱལ་མ་སྤངས་མཉམ་ཉིད་ཡེ་ཤེས་སོ། །
NGAGYAL MAPANG NYAMNYI YESHE SO
Without denying pride, it is liberated as the wisdom of equality.

རང་ལས་ཆེ་བའི་གཞན་གྱི་སྟོབས་འབྱོར་དང་། །
RANG LÉ CHEWÉ SHEN GYI TOBJOR DANG
Think about the wealth and power of others who are greater than you.

ཡོན་ཏན་མཁན་དང་གདུལ་བྱ་མང་བ་དང་། །
YÖNTEN KHEN DANG DÜLJA MANGWA DANG
How knowledgeable they are, their many qualities and social circles,

རིག་གནས་མཁས་དང་འདོན་བཟང་སྐད་བཟང་དང་། །
RIGNÉ KHÉ DANG DÖN ZANG KÉ ZANG DANG
Their skill as a scholar, their excellent chanting, their good voice,

ཆོས་ཀྱི་གོ་བ་འཇིག་རྟེན་གཏམ་ལ་སོགས། །
CHÖ KYI GOWA JIKTEN TAM LA SOK
Their understanding of Dharma, worldly talk, etc.

Song 13 - Self Liberation of Five Toxins

གཞན་གྱི་ཡོན་ཏན་ཐམས་ཅད་བསམ་བྱས་ནས། །
SHEN GYI YÖNTEN TAMCHÉ SAM JÉ NÉ
Thinking about all the good qualities of others (social media comparison),

རང་ལས་མཐོ་བར་དོགས་པའི་ཕྲག་དོག་སེམས། །
RANG LÉ THOWAR DOKPÉ THRAKDOK SEM
Feeling that others are better than yourself, the jealous mind arises,

སྐྱེར་ཆུག་སྐྱེས་ཚེ་ཕྲག་དོག་ངོ་བོ་ལ། །
KYERCHUK KYÉ TSÉ THRAKDOK NGOWO LA
When strong jealousy arises, look directly at its essence.

ཅེར་གྱིས་ལྟོས་ལ་ཕྲག་དོག་མཁན་པོ་དེ། །
CHER GYI TÖ LA THRAKDOK KHENPO DÉ
Look intently at the projector of jealousy.

དང་པོ་གང་ནས་བྱུང་དང་ད་ལྟའི་དུས། །
DANGPO GANG NÉ JUNG DANG DA TI DÜ
Where did it come from in the beginning?

གང་དུ་གནས་དང་ཐ་མ་གང་དུ་འགྲོ། །
GANG DU NÉ DANG THAMA GANG DU DRO
Where does it abide now? And where will it go in the end?

དབྱིབས་དང་ཁ་དོག་ལ་སོགས་ཨེ་འདུག་ལྟོས། །
YIB DANG KHADOK LASOK É DUK TÖ
Look to see if it has a shape, color, etc.

བལྟས་ཚེ་ཡེ་ནས་སྟོང་པ་འཛིན་མེད་ཡིན། །
TÉ TSÉ YENÉ TONGPA DZINMÉ YIN
When you look, it is primordially empty and without grasping.

ཕྲག་དོག་མ་སྤངས་བྱ་གྲུབ་ཡེ་ཤེས་སོ། །
THRAKDOK MAPANG JA DRUB YESHE SO
Without denying jealousy, it is liberated as all-accomplishing wisdom.

དེ་ལྟར་རྟོགས་ན་ཉོན་མོངས་ཡེ་ཤེས་ཡིན། །
DETAR TOK NA NYÖNMONG YESHE YIN
If you understand in that way, the afflictions themselves are wisdom.

ཉོན་མོངས་རྟོག་པ་སྤངས་པའི་ཕ་རོལ་ནས། །
NYÖNMONG TOKPA PANGPÉ PHAROL NÉ
By abandoning afflictive thoughts,

སྟོང་ཉིད་ཡེ་ཤེས་འཚོལ་བ་དགོད་རེ་བྲོ། །
TONGNYI YESHE TSÖLWA GÖ RÉ DRO
Searching for the wisdom of emptiness is laughable.

བཙལ་བས་མ་རྙེད་ཚེ་ན་སྙིང་རེ་རྗེ། །
TSALWÉ MA NYÉ TSÉ NA NYING RÉ JÉ
If you search and do not find it, it is pitiable.

འདི་ལྟར་དུག་ལྔ་སྟོང་པར་ཤེས་ནས་ཀྱང་། །
DITAR DUK NGA TONGPAR SHÉ NÉ KYANG
Having understood the five mental toxins as empty in this way,

ཕྱིན་ཆད་དུག་ལྔའི་རྟོག་པ་གང་ཤར་ཡང་། །
CHINCHÉ DUK NGÉ TOKPA GANG SHAR YANG
From now on, whatever mental arising of the five mental toxins occurs,

Song 13 - Self Liberation of Five Toxins

དོ་སྟོད་འདི་བཞིན་སྐྱེ་ས་གནས་ས་དང་། །
NGÖTRO DIBZHIN KYÉSA NÉSA DANG
After this introduction — regarding its origin, location,

འགྲོ་ས་དབྱིབས་དང་ཁ་དོག་དཔྱད་མི་དགོས། །
DROSA YIB DANG KHADOK PÉ MI GÖ
where it goes, its shape, or color — you don't need to analyze,

སྔོན་དུ་དུག་ལྔ་སྟོང་པར་ཤེས་པའི་ཕྱིར། །
NGÖN DU DUK NGA TONGPAR SHÉPÉ CHIR
Because you have already understood the five mental toxins as empty.

ཤར་མ་ཐག་ཏུ་རྗེས་སུ་མི་འབྲང་བར། །
SHAR MATHAK TU JÉSU MI DRANGWAR
As soon as they arise, without chasing after them,

སེམས་ཉིད་ངང་དུ་རང་སར་གློད་ལ་ཞོག །
SEMNYI NGANG DU RANGSAR LÖ LA SHOK
Release and rest your own mind naturally in its own place.

རང་ཡལ་ཉིད་དུ་འགྲོ་བར་ཐེ་ཚོམ་མེད། །
RANG YAL NYI DU DROWAR THÉTSOM MÉ
There is no doubt that they will naturally self-evaporate.

འདི་ནི་དོ་སྟོད་རྩལ་སྦྱོང་གཉིས་ཀ་ཡིན། །
DI NI NGÖTRO TSAL JONG NYI KA YIN
This is both a pointing out and a skill to practice.

འདི་ལྟར་སྔོན་ལ་རྩལ་སྦྱོང་བྱས་གྱུར་ན། །
DITAR NGÖN LA TSAL JONG JÉ GYUR NA
If you have already trained in this way,

ཕྱིན་ཆད་ཉོན་མོངས་དུག་ལྔ་རྣམ་ཤར་ཚེ། །
CHINCHÉ NYÖNMONG DUK NGA NAM SHAR TSÉ
From now on, whenever the five mental toxins arise,

ཉོན་མོངས་རང་མཚང་སྔོན་ལ་ཤེས་ཐབས་ཀྱིས། །
NYÖNMONG RANG TSANG NGÖN LA SHÉ TAB KYI
Due to having seen the true nature of afflictions,

སྟོང་ཉིད་ཡེ་ཤེས་གཉིས་ཀ་མཉམ་ཤར་ནས། །
TONGNYI YESHE NYI KA NYAM SHAR NÉ
Emptiness and wisdom will arise simultaneously.

ཤར་གྲོལ་དུས་མཉམ་ཤར་གྲོལ་དུས་མཉམ་མོ། །
SHAR DROL DÜ NYAM SHAR DROL DÜ NYAMMO
Arising and liberation are simultaneous! Arising and liberation are indeed simultaneous!

བླ་མ་གོང་མའི་རྣམ་ཐར་གསུང་རྒྱུན་དུ། །
LAMA GONGMÉ NAMTHAR SUNG GYÜN DU
In the biographies and oral traditions of the past gurus,

ཉོན་མོངས་རྟོག་པ་མང་ན་ཆོས་སྐུ་མང་། །
NYÖNMONG TOKPA MANG NA CHÖ KU MANG
It is said, "The more afflictive thoughts, the more Dharmakaya."

གསུངས་པ་ཇི་བཞིན་ཡིན་པས་ཤེས་པར་གྱིས། །
SUNGPA JIZHIN YIN PÉ SHÉPAR GYI
Understand that this is exactly as it is said.

Song 13 - Self Liberation of Five Toxins

ལས་ནི་དང་པོ་བ་ལ་ཉོན་མོངས་སེམས། །
LÉ NI DANGPO WA LA NYÖNMONG SEM
For beginners, when afflictive emotions arise strongly,

ཤུག་དྲག་ཤར་ཚེ་དཔྱད་འཇོག་བྱས་ན་བཟང་། །
SHUK DRAK SHAR TSÉ PÉ JOK JÉ NA ZANG
It is good to analyze and then rest [12].

འདི་ནི་ཞལ་ཤེས་ཡིན་པས་ཐུགས་ལ་ཞོག །
DI NI SHALSHE YIN PÉ THUK LA SHOK
Keep this in your mind, as it is an oral instruction.

འདི་ནི་དུག་ལྔ་རང་གྲོལ་རོ་སྟོད་དོ།། །།
DI NI DUK NGA RANGDROL NGÖTRO DO
This is the introduction to the self-liberation of five mental toxins.

---

12. Alternating between **shamatha** (calm abiding, Tibetan: *shiné* ཞི་གནས་) and **vipassana** (analytic meditation, Tibetan: *lhaktong* ལྷག་མཐོང་).

SONG 14

Self Liberation of Six Sensorial Experiences

ཧཱུྃ ཨེ་མ་ཧོ། ད་ཡང་སྙིང་དང་འདྲ་བའི་བུ་རྣམས་ཉོན། །
EMAHO DA YANG NYING DANG DRA WÉ BU NAM NYÖN
Emaho! Now again, you who are like my heart, listen!

གོས་ལ་སོགས་པའི་འཇམ་པོ་ལུས་ལ་དྲིལ། །
GÖ LASOK PÉ JAMPO LÜ LA DRIL
Touch or wear something soft, like clothes,

འཇམ་མོ་སྙམ་པའི་རང་གི་སེམས་ལ་ལྟོས། །
JAMPO NYAMPA'I RANG GI SEM LA TÖ
Look at your own mind thinking, "It's soft."

རེ་བ་ལ་སོགས་རྩུབ་མོ་ལུས་ལ་དྲིལ། །
REWA LASOK TSÜBO LÜ LA DRIL
Touch or wear something rough, like burlap,

རྩུབ་པོ་སྙམ་པའི་རང་གི་སེམས་ལ་ལྟོས། །
TSÜBO NYAMPA'I RANG GI SEM LA TÖ
Look at your own mind thinking, "It's rough."

Song 14 - Self Liberation of Six Sensorial Experiences

བལྟས་ཚེ་གཉིས་ཀ་སྟོང་པར་རོ་མཉམ་མོ། །
TÉ TSÉ NYI KA TONGPAR RO NYAMMO
When you look, both are equal in emptiness.

གསེར་སྐུ་ལ་སོགས་མཛེས་པའི་གཟུགས་ལ་ལྟོས། །
SERKU LASOK DZEPÉ ZUK LA TÖ
Look at a beautiful form, like a golden statue
(or anything you enjoy seeing),

མཛེས་སོ་སྙམ་པའི་རང་གི་སེམས་ལ་ལྟོས། །
DZÉ SO NYAMPA'I RANG GI SEM LA TÖ
Look at your own mind thinking, "It's beautiful."

སྦལ་པ་ལ་སོགས་མི་མཛེས་གཟུགས་ལ་ལྟོས། །
BALPA LASOK MINDZÉ ZUK LA TÖ
Look at an ugly form (like a toad, or something ugly for you),

མི་མཛེས་སྙམ་པའི་རང་གི་སེམས་ལ་ལྟོས། །
MINDZÉ NYAMPA'I RANG GI SEM LA TÖ
Look at your own mind thinking, "It's ugly."

བལྟས་ཚེ་གཉིས་ཀ་སྟོང་པར་རོ་མཉམ་མོ། །
TÉ TSÉ NYI KA TONGPAR RO NYAMMO
When you look, both are equal in emptiness.

བུ་རམ་ལ་སོགས་ཞིམ་པོ་ཁ་རུ་ཟོ། །
BURAM LASOK ZHIMPO KHA RU ZO
Eat something delicious, like molasses (or anything sweet),

མངར་རོ་སྙམ་པའི་རང་གི་སེམས་ལ་ལྟོས། །
NGARRO NYAMPA'I RANG GI SEM LA TÖ
Look at your own mind thinking, "It's sweet."

བཅའ་སྒ་ལ་སོགས་ཁ་རུ་མྱངས་ནས་ཀྱང་། །
CHALGA LASOK KHA RU NYANG NÉ KYANG
Taste something strong (like ginger),

ཁ་ཁ་མྱམ་པའི་རང་གི་སེམས་ལ་ལྟོས། །
KHAKHA NYAMPA'I RANG GI SEM LA TÖ
Look at your own mind thinking, "It's bitter." or "hot"

བལྟས་ཚེ་གཉིས་ཀ་སྟོང་པར་རོ་མཉམ་མོ། །
TÉ TSÉ NYI KA TONGPAR RO NYAMMO
When you look, both are equal in emptiness.

ཙན་དན་སྤོས་སོགས་དྲི་ནི་ཞིམ་པོར་སྣོམས། །
TSENDEN PÖ SOK DRI NI ZHIMPOR NOM
Smell a pleasant scent like sandalwood incense
(or any good perfume),

ཞིམ་མོ་མྱམ་པའི་རང་གི་སེམས་ལ་ལྟོས། །
ZHIMMO NYAMPA'I RANG GI SEM LA TÖ
Look at your own mind thinking, "It's pleasant."

ཤིང་ཀུན་སྒོག་པ་ལ་སོགས་དྲི་ངན་སྣོམས། །
SHINGKÜN GOKPA LASOK DRIN GEN NOM
Smell a bad scent like asafoetida, garlic, (or any smell you dislike),

མི་ཞིམ་མྱམ་པའི་རང་གི་སེམས་ལ་ལྟོས། །
MIZHIM NYAMPA'I RANG GI SEM LA TÖ
Look at your own mind thinking, "It's unpleasant."

Song 14 - Self Liberation of Six Sensorial Experiences

བལྟས་ཚེ་གཉིས་ཀ་སྟོང་པར་རོ་མཉམ་མོ། །
TÉ TSÉ NYI KA TONGPAR RO NYAMMO
When you look, both are equal in emptiness.

དྲིལ་བུ་པི་ཝང་གླིང་བུའི་སྒྲ་ལ་ཉོན། །
DRILBU PIWANG LINGBÜ DRA LA NYÖN
Listen to the sound of a bell, a lute, or flute (or any enjoyable sound)

སྙན་ནོ་སྙམ་པའི་རང་གི་སེམས་ལ་ལྟོས། །
NYEN NO NYAMPA'I RANG GI SEM LA TÖ
Look at your own mind thinking, "It's pleasant."

རྡོ་དང་ཐལ་མོ་རྡོབ་ལ་སྒྲ་ལ་ཉོན། །
DO DANG THALMO DOB LA DRA LA NYÖN
Listen to the sound of stones smashing or hands clapping (
or loud traffic or construction noises),

མི་སྙན་སྙམ་པའི་རང་གི་སེམས་ལ་ལྟོས། །
MINYEN NYAMPA'I RANG GI SEM LA TÖ
Look at your own mind thinking, "It's unpleasant."

བལྟས་ཚེ་གཉིས་ཀ་སྟོང་པར་རོ་མཉམ་མོ། །
TÉ TSÉ NYI KA TONGPAR RO NYAMMO
When you look, both are equal in emptiness.

ཁྱེད་རྣམས་གླིང་བཞིའི་ཁམས་ལ་དབང་བསྒྱུར་བའི། །
KHYERANG LING ZHI KHAM LA WANG GYURWÉ
Imagine that you have become a universal monarch ruling over the four continents.

འཁོར་ལོས་བསྒྱུར་རྒྱལ་ཞིག་ཏུ་སྐྱེས་ནས་ཀྱང་། །
KHORLÖ GYURGYAL SHYIK TU KYÉ NÉ KYANG
Having been born as a universal monarch,

བཙུན་མོ་བློན་པོ་མང་པོའི་འཁོར་གྱིས་བསྐོར། །
TSÜNMO LÖNPO MANGPÖ KHOR GYI KOR
Surrounded by a retinue of many consorts and ministers,

རིན་ཆེན་སྣ་ལྔ་ལས་གྲུབ་ཁང་པ་ན། །
RINCHEN NA NGA LÉ DRUB KHANGPA NA
In a palace made of the five precious jewels,

རོ་བརྒྱ་ལྡན་པའི་ཁ་ཟས་ཟ་བར་སྒོམས། །
RO GYA DENPÉ KHAZÉ ZAWAR GOM
Meditate on eating food with a hundred flavors.

དེ་འདྲའི་སྣང་བ་སེམས་ལ་ཤར་བའི་ཚེ། །
DI DRA'I NANGWA SEM LA SHARWÉ TSÉ
When such imaginations arise in your mind,

བདེ་འོ་སྙམ་པའི་རང་གི་སེམས་ལ་ལྟོས། །
DEO NYAMPA'I RANG GI SEM LA TÖ
Look at your own mind thinking, "It's happiness."

ཁྱེད་རྣམས་དབུལ་པོ་འཁོར་གཡོག་གཅིག་ཀྱང་མེད། །
KHYERANG ULPO KHORGYOK CHIK KYANG MÉ
Then imagine that you are extremely poor, without even one friend.

གྱང་ར་ཞིག་པོ་ཞིག་ཏུ་མལ་བཅས་ནས། །
GYANGRA SHYIKPO SHYIK TU MAL CHÉ NÉ
Having made your bed in an old dilapidated ruin,

Song 14 - Self Liberation of Six Sensorial Experiences

སྟེང་ནས་ཆར་བབ་འོག་ནས་སས་བརྫུན་ཅིང་། །
TENG NÉ CHARBAB OK NÉ SÉ LEN CHING
With rain falling from above and the ground wet from below,

ལུས་ལ་མཛེ་སོགས་ནད་སྣ་མང་པོས་བཏབ། །
LÜ LA DZÉ SOK NÉ NA MANGPÖ TAB
Your body afflicted by many kinds of illnesses, like leprosy,
(or a skin infection)

རྐང་ལག་ཆད་ནས་སྡུག་བསྔལ་དུ་མ་ཡིས། །
KANGLAK CHÉ NÉ DUKNGAL DUMA YI
With your legs and arms cut off, tormented by various sufferings,

མནར་ནས་སྡུག་བསྔལ་མྱོང་བ་ཞིག་ཏུ་སྒོམས། །
NAR NÉ DUKNGAL NYONGWA SHYIK TU GOM
Meditate on the experience of intense suffering.

དེ་འདྲའི་སྣང་བ་ཡིད་ལ་ཤར་བའི་ཚེ། །
DI DRA'I NANGWA YI LA SHARWÉ TSÉ
When such imaginations arise in your mind,

སྡུག་གོ་སྙམ་པའི་རང་གི་སེམས་ལ་ལྟོས། །
DUK GO NYAMPA'I RANG GI SEM LA TÖ
Look at your own mind thinking, "It's suffering."

བལྟས་ཚེ་བདེ་སྡུག་སྟོང་པར་རོ་མཉམ་མོ། །
TÉ TSÉ DEDUK TONGPAR RO NYAMMO
When you look, happiness and suffering are equal in emptiness.

The Flight of Garuda

འདི་ལྟར་ཚོགས་དྲུག་སྟོང་པར་ཤེས་ནས་ཀྱང་། །
DITAR TSOK DRUK TONGPAR SHÉ NÉ KYANG
Having understood the six collections (of senses and their objects) as empty in this way.

ཕྱིན་ཆད་ཚོགས་དྲུག་བཟང་ངན་གང་ཤར་ཚེ། །
CHINCHÉ TSOK DRUK ZANG NGEN GANG SHAR TSÉ
From now on, whenever anything good or bad arises in the six senses,

དོ་སྟོད་འདི་བཞིན་དཔྱད་པ་མི་དགོས་ཏེ། །
NGÖTRO DIBZHIN PÉPA MI GÖ TÉ
You don't need to analyze like you did with this introduction,

གཞི་མེད་ཡེ་གྲོལ་སྟོང་པ་ཡིན་པའི་ཕྱིར། །
SHYIMÉ YEDROL TONGPA YINPÉ CHIR
Because they are baseless, primordially liberated, and empty.

ཤར་ཙམ་ཉིད་ནས་རྗེས་སུ་མི་འབྲང་བར། །
SHAR TSAM NYI NÉ JÉSU MI DRANGWAR
From the moment they arise, without following after them,

སེམས་ཉིད་ངང་དུ་རང་སར་གློད་ལ་ཞོག །
SEMNYI NGANG DU RANGSAR LÖ LA SHOK
Release and rest your own mind naturally in its own place.

རང་གྲོལ་ཉིད་དུ་འགྲོ་བར་ཐེ་ཚོམ་མེད། །
RANGDROL NYI DU DROWAR THÉTSOM MÉ
There is no doubt that they will be self-liberated.

Song 14 - Self Liberation of Six Sensorial Experiences

འདི་ནི་ཚོགས་དྲུག་རང་གྲོལ་ངོ་སྤྲོད་དོ། །

DI NI TSOK DRUK RANGDROL NGÖTRO DO

This is the introduction to the self-liberation of the six sensorial experiences.

SONG 15

Stillness, Motion, Awareness

ཀྱཻ ཨེ་མ་ཧོ། ད་ཡང་རིགས་ཀྱི་བུ་རྣམས་ལེགས་པར་ཉོན། །
EMAHO DA YANG RIK KYI BU NAM LEKPAR NYÖN
Emaho! Now again, you of noble lineage, listen well!

ཁྱེད་རྣམས་རང་སེམས་བློད་ལ་རང་བབས་སུ། །
KHYERANG RANGSEM LÖ LA RANGBAB SU
Relax your own mind and let it be natural.

ཞོག་ལ་ཇི་ལྟར་གནས་པའི་ཚུལ་ལ་ལྟོས། །
SHOK LA JITAR NÉ PÉ TSUL LA TÖ
Rest and look at how it abides.

བལྟས་ཚེ་རིག་པའི་ངང་ལ་གནས་པའི་ཕྱིར། །
TÉ TSÉ RIGPÉ NGANG LA NÉ PÉ CHIR
When you look, it abides in the state of awareness.

གནས་ཀྱང་སྟོང་པ་རིག་པའི་ངང་ཡིན་པས། །
NÉ KYANG TONGPA RIGPÉ NGANG YIN PÉ
When it abides, it is empty in the state of awareness.

Song 15 - Stillness, Motion, Awareness

སྐལ་ལྡན་སེམས་ཀྱི་བུ་རྣམས་ཤེས་པར་གྱིས། །
KALDEN SEM KYI BU NAM SHÉPAR GYI
Fortunate children of my heart, understand this!

གནས་པ་སེམས་ཀྱི་རྒྱན་དུ་ངོ་སྤྲོད་དོ། །
NÉ PA SEM KYI GYEN DU NGÖTRO DO
This is the introduction to the abiding state as the ornament of mind.

རྣམ་རྟོག་སྤྲོས་ལ་ཇི་ལྟར་འཕྲོ་ཚུལ་ལ། །
NAMTOK TRÖ LA JITAR THRO TSUL LA
Let conceptual thoughts arise, look at how they move.

སྟོང་དང་སྟོང་གསལ་རིག་པའི་ངང་ཉིད་ལས། །
TÖ DANG TONGSAL RIGPÉ NGANG NYI LÉ
Look from this very state of empty clear awareness.

ཅུང་ཟད་ཙམ་ཡང་གཡོ་བ་མེད་པའི་ཕྱིར། །
CHUNGZÉ TSAM YANG YOWA MEPÉ CHIR
Since there is no wavering whatsoever,

འཕྲོ་ཡང་སྟོང་པ་རིག་པའི་ངང་ཡིན་པས། །
THRO YANG TONGPA RIGPÉ NGANG YIN PÉ
Even when they arise, they are empty in the state of awareness.

སྐལ་ལྡན་རིགས་ཀྱི་བུ་རྣམས་ཤེས་པར་གྱིས། །
KALDEN RIK KYI BU NAM SHÉPAR GYI
Fortunate children of noble lineage, understand this!

འཕྲོ་བ་སེམས་ཀྱི་རོལ་པར་ངོ་སྤྲོད་དོ། །
THRO WA SEM KYI ROLPAR NGÖTRO DO
This is the introduction to the arising state as the play of mind.

The Flight of Garuda

དཔེར་ན་རྒྱ་མཚོར་བ་རླབས་ཅི་ཤར་ཡང་། །
PER NA GYATSOR BAR LAB CHI SHAR YANG
For example, whatever waves arise in the ocean,

རྒྱ་མཚོ་ཉིད་ལས་ཅུང་ཟད་མ་གཡོས་ལྟར། །
GYATSO NYI LÉ CHUNGZÉ MA YÖ TAR
Just as they do not move even slightly from the ocean itself,

སེམས་ནི་གནས་སམ་འགྱུ་ཡང་རིག་སྟོང་དང་། །
SEM NI NÉ SAM GYU YANG RIKTONG DANG
Mind, whether still or moving, is awareness and emptiness;

ཅུང་ཟད་ཙམ་ཡང་གཡོ་བ་མེད་པའི་ཕྱིར། །
CHUNGZÉ TSAM YANG YOWA MEPÉ CHIR
There is not even the slightest movement from this.

གང་ལྟར་གནས་ཀྱང་རིག་པའི་ངང་ཡིན་ཤོག །
GANGTAR NÉ KYANG RIGPÉ NGANG YIN SHOK
However it abides, let it be the state of awareness.

གང་ལྟར་ཤར་ཡང་རིག་པའི་གདངས་ཡིན་ཤོག །
GANGTAR SHAR YANG RIGPÉ DANG YIN SHOK
However it arises, let it be the radiance of awareness.

སེམས་ནི་གནས་ན་སྒོམ་ནི་ཡིན་པར་འདོད། །
SEM NI NÉ NA GOM NI YINPAR DÖ
As for the mind, when it abides, one thinks "This is meditation."

འཕྲོ་ན་སྒོམ་ནི་མིན་པར་འདོད་པ་དེ། །
THRO NA GOM NI MINPAR DÖPA DÉ
When it arises (with thoughts and emotions), one thinks, "this is not meditation."

Song 15 - Stillness, Motion, Awareness

གནས་འགྱུ་གཉིས་ཀྱི་རང་མཚང་མ་ཤེས་པར། །
NÉ GYU NYI KYI RANG TSANG MA SHÉPAR
This is due to not knowing the deep nature of abiding and arising.

གནས་འགྱུ་རིག་གསུམ་གཅིག་ཏུ་མ་འདྲེས་རྟགས། །
NÉ GYU RIK SUM CHIK TU MA DRÉ TAK
Seeing them as separate is a sign that abiding, arising,
and awareness have not merged into one.

དེ་ཕྱིར་སྐལ་ལྡན་སེམས་ཀྱི་བུ་མཆོག་ཀུན། །
DÉ CHIR KALDEN SEM KYI BU CHOK KÜN
Therefore, all fortunate, supreme children of my heart,

གནས་རུང་འགྱུ་རུང་རིག་པའི་ངང་ཡིན་པས། །
NÉ RUNG GYU RUNG RIGPÉ NGANG YIN PÉ
Whether it abides or arises, since it is only the state of awareness,

འདི་རྣམས་སྔོན་ལ་ཐུགས་སུ་ཆུད་ནས་ཀྱང་། །
DI NAM NGÖN LA THUK SU CHÜ NÉ KYANG
First, having understood this in your heart,

གནས་འགྱུ་རིག་གསུམ་གཅིག་ཏུ་ཉམས་སུ་ལོངས། །
NÉ GYU RIK SUM CHIK TU NYAM SU LONG
Experience stillness, motion, and awareness as one.

འཕྲོ་གནས་གཉིས་སུ་མེད་པར་ངོ་སྤྲོད་དོ། །
THRO NÉ NYISU MEPAR NGÖTRO DO
This is the introduction to abiding and arising as being non-dual.

The Flight of Garuda

SONG 16

One Taste

ཀྱེ་ཨེ་མ་ཧོ། སྐལ་བར་ལྡན་པའི་སེམས་ཀྱི་བུ་གཅིག་པོ། །
EMAHO KALWAR DENPÉ SEM KYI BU CHIKPO
Emaho! Child of my heart who has good fortune,

ཁྱེད་རྣམས་མ་ཡེངས་དལ་ལེ་རྣ་བས་ཉོན། །
KHYERANG MAYENG DAL LÉ NAWÉ NYÖN
Do not be distracted, stay relaxed and listen!

སྒུ་པ་བྱ་བཏང་ཚོགས་དྲུག་རང་གྲོལ་ངས། །
LUPA JATANG TSOK DRUK RANGDROL NGE
I, the carefree singer, Tsodruk Rangdrol,

གླུ་དབྱངས་སྙན་མོ་གངས་དཀར་སེམས་ལ་འཇོག །
LUDYANG NYENMO GANGKAR SEM LA JOK
Will place a melodious song in the mind that is as pure as white snow.

ཆོས་རྣམས་ཐམས་ཅད་རོ་གཅིག་སྟོང་པ་རུ། །
CHÖ NAM TAMCHÉ RO CHIK TONGPA RU
All dharmas are of one taste in emptiness.

གཏན་ལ་ཕེབས་ན་འཁོར་འདས་སྤང་བླང་བྲལ། །
TEN LA PHEB NA KHORDÉ PANGLANG DRAL
If you arrive at this final point, samsara and nirvana are free from both abandoning and adopting.

དགྲ་དང་གཉེན་དུ་འཛིན་པའི་འཁྲུལ་པ་འཇིག །
DRA DANG NYEN DU DZINPÉ THRULPA JIK
The delusion of holding onto enemies and friends will be destroyed.

བདག་གཞན་གཉིས་སུ་འཛིན་པའི་སྣང་བ་མེད། །
DAK SHEN NYISU DZINPÉ NANGWA MÉ
The appearance of holding self and other as separate will not exist.

ཐམས་ཅད་རོ་གཅིག་སྟོང་པར་རྟོགས་ཕྱིར་རོ། །
TAMCHÉ RO CHIK TONGPAR TOK CHIR RO
The realization that everything is of one taste in emptiness will dawn.

རྒྱས་བཤད་མདོ་འགག་ཏུ་ན་འདི་ཡིན་ཏེ། །
GYASHÉ DO GAK DU NA DI YIN TÉ
If the extensive explanations are condensed to their crucial point, this is it:

ཐེག་པའི་ཡང་རྩེ་རྫོགས་པ་ཆེན་པོ་རུ། །
THEKPÉ YANGTSÉ DZOGPA CHENPO RU
In Dzogchen, the very peak of all vehicles,

འཁོར་བ་མྱང་འདས་ཐམས་ཅད་གཞི་རྩ་བྲལ། །
KHORWA NYANGDÉ TAMCHÉ SHYITSA DRAL
All of samsara and nirvana are without a fundamental root.

Song 16 - One Taste

ཡེ་ནས་སངས་རྒྱས་ཆོས་སྐུར་རོ་གཅིག་གོ །

YENÉ SANGGYÉ CHÖ KUR RO CHIK GO

From the very beginning, enlightened and one taste as Dharmakaya.

རྫོགས་ཆེན་ངང་ལ་ལྷ་འདྲེ་གཉིས་སུ་མེད། །

DZOGCHEN NGANG LA LHA DRÉ NYI SU MÉ

In the nature of Dzogchen, gods and demons are not two.

རྫོགས་ཆེན་ཡུལ་ལ་སངས་རྒྱས་སེམས་ཅན་མེད། །

DZOGCHEN YÜL LA SANGGYÉ SEMCHEN MÉ

In the realm of Dzogchen, there are no Buddhas and sentient beings.

རྫོགས་ཆེན་གཞི་ལ་བཟང་དང་ངན་པ་མེད། །

DZOGCHEN ZHI LA ZANG DANG NGENPA MÉ

In the ground of Dzogchen, there is no good and bad.

རྫོགས་ཆེན་ལམ་ལ་ཉེ་དང་རིང་བ་མེད། །

DZOGCHEN LAM LA NYÉ DANG RINGWA MÉ

On the path of Dzogchen, there is no slow and fast.

རྫོགས་ཆེན་འབྲས་བུར་ཐོབ་དང་མ་ཐོབ་མེད། །

DZOGCHEN DREBU THOB DANG MATHOB MÉ

In the result of Dzogchen, there is no achieving and not achieving.

རྫོགས་ཆེན་ཆོས་ལ་སྤྱོད་དང་མི་སྤྱོད་མེད། །

DZOGCHEN CHÖ LA CHÖ DANG MICHÖ MÉ

In the Dharma of Dzogchen, there is no practicing and not practicing.

The Flight of Garuda

རྫོགས་ཆེན་དོན་ལ་སྒོམ་དང་མི་སྒོམ་མེད། །
DZOGCHEN DÖN LA GOM DANG MIGOM MÉ
In the meaning of Dzogchen, there is no meditating and not meditating.

རྫོགས་ཆེན་རྒྱལ་པོའི་ལྟ་བ་དེ་བཞིན་གནས། །
DZOGCHEN GYALPÖ TAWA DEZHIN NÉ
The royal view of Dzogchen is just this way.

དེ་འདྲའི་རྫོགས་ཆེན་ལྟ་བ་རྟོགས་པའི་ཚེ། །
DI DRA'I DZOGCHEN TAWA TOKPÉ TSÉ
When you realize such a Dzogchen view,

སྒོ་གསུམ་ཕྲ་རགས་རྟོགས་པ་ཀུན་ཞི་ནས། །
GO SUM PHRA RAK TOKPA KÜN ZHI NÉ
All the subtle and gross understandings of the three doors of body, speech, and mind are at peace.

དཔེར་ན་བལ་ལ་ཆུ་བཏབ་ཇི་བཞིན་དུ། །
PER NA BAL LA CHU TAB JIZHIN DU
For example, just like water poured on wool,

སྒོ་གསུམ་ཞི་ཞིང་དུལ་བའི་ངང་ལ་གནས། །
GO SUM ZHI ZHING DULWÉ NGANG LA NÉ
The three doors remain in a state which is soft and gentle.

བདེ་གསལ་མི་རྟོགས་ཏིང་འཛིན་སྐྱེ་བ་དང་། །
DESAL MITOK TINGDZIN KYEWA DANG
When the samadhi of bliss, clarity and non-conceptuality arises,

དེ་ལྟར་མ་རྟོགས་འཁོར་འཁྱམས་འགྲོ་ཀུན་ལ། །
DETAR MATOK KHOR KHYAM DRO KÜN LA
To all those wandering beings who have not realized that way,

མ་ཡིས་བུ་གཅིག་དག་ལ་བརྩེ་བ་ལྟར། །
MA YI BU CHIK DAK LA TSEWA TAR
Just like a mother's love for her only child,

བཅོས་མིན་སྙིང་རྗེ་སྐྱེ་བ་རྫོགས་ཆེན་གྱི། །
CHÖMIN NYINGJÉ KYEWA DZOGCHEN GYI
Unfabricated compassion arises — This is the characteristic of Dzogchen.

ལྟ་བའི་ཁྱད་ཆོས་ཡིན་པའང་ཤེས་པར་གྱིས། །
TAWÉ KHYENCHÖ YINPA'ANG SHÉPAR GYI
Know that this is also a special quality of the view.

ཐམས་ཅད་སྟོང་པ་ཉིད་དུ་ཐག་བཅད་ནས། །
TAMCHÉ TONGPA NYI DU TAKCHÉ NÉ
Having decided that everything is emptiness,

དགེ་སྤང་སྡིག་ལ་འཛེམ་མེད་སྤྱོད་གྱུར་ན། །
GE PANG DIK LA DZEMMÉ CHÖ GYUR NA
If you engage in abandoning virtue and readily practicing negativity,

ནག་པོ་ཁ་འཇམས་བདུད་ཀྱི་ལྟ་བ་སྟེ། །
NAKPO KHAJAM DÜ KYI TAWA TÉ
You are under the demonic influence of wrong views.

The Flight of Garuda

དེ་འདྲའི་བདུད་ལྟའི་དབང་དུ་མ་ཤོར་གཅེས། །
DI DRAI DÜD TI WANG DU MA SHOR CHÉ
Do not fall under the power of such a harmful view,

འདི་རྣམས་རྫོགས་པ་ཆེན་པོའི་རྡོ་སྟོད་དོ། །
DI NAM DZOGPA CHENPÖ NGÖTRO DO
These are the pointers of Dzogpa Chenpo.

རྡོ་སྟོད་འདི་རྣམས་ཤིན་ཏུ་གལ་ཆེ་སྟེ། །
NGÖTRO DI NAM SHINTU GALCHÉ TÉ
These introductions are extremely important.

ཕྱི་རོལ་ཀུན་རྫོབ་སྣང་གྲག་ཆོས་རྣམས་ཀུན། །
CHIROL KÜNDZOB NANGDRAK CHÖ NAM KÜN
All external, relative appearances, sounds, and phenomena,

ཐམས་ཅད་སྟོང་པ་ཉིད་དུ་མ་རྟོགས་པར། །
TAMCHÉ TONGPA NYI DU MA TOKPAR
Without realizing they are all emptiness,

ལྟ་བ་བསྒོམ་ན་སྙམ་ཡང་ཅི་ཞིག་སྒོམ། །
TAWA GOM NA NYAM YANG CHISHIK GOM
If you think you are meditating on the view, what exactly are you meditating on?

དེ་ཡི་ཕྱིར་ན་དང་པོ་འདི་ལྟར་དུ། །
DÉ YI CHIR NA DANGPO DITAR DU
Therefore, in the beginning, in this way,

རེ་འགའ་བླ་མར་གསོལ་བ་འདེབས་ཀྱིན་སྟོབས། །
RE GA LAMA SOLWA DEB KYIN TÖ
Sometimes observe while praying to the guru (Guru Yoga),

Song 16 - One Taste

རེ་འགའ་གློད་ཀྱིན་སྒྲིམ་ཀྱིན་ལེགས་པར་ལྟོས། །
RE GA LÖ KYIN DRIM KYIN LEKPAR TÖ
Sometimes observe while relaxing, and sometimes while being focused.

དེ་ལྟར་བལྟས་ཚེ་སེམས་ལ་དགའ་བ་དང་། །
DE TAR TÉ TSÉ SEM LA GAWA DANG
When you observe in that way, with happiness in the mind,

ཐམས་ཅད་སྟོང་པ་ཉིད་དུ་ལམ་ལམ་དུ། །
TAMCHÉ TONGPA NYI DU LAMLAM DU
Everything will manifest clearly as the very nature of emptiness,

ཤར་ནས་ཕྱི་རོལ་སྣང་བའི་ཡུལ་རྣམས་ལ། །
SHAR NÉ CHIROL NANGWÉ YÜL NAM LA
When you have this inner certainty, then regardless of outer appearing objects,

ལག་པས་རེག་ཀྱང་འཛིན་རྒྱུ་མེད་ཉམས་དང་། །
LAKPÉ REK KYANG DZIN GYU MÉ NYAM DANG
Even if you touch them with your hand, you will feel there is nothing to grasp.

ལྟ་བ་འདི་ཉིད་ངེས་པར་ཡིན་པར་འདུག །
TAWA DI NYI NGEPAR YINPAR DUK
Thinking that this very view is definitely true,

སྙམ་པའི་ངེས་ཤེས་གཏིང་ཚུགས་སྐྱེ་བར་ངེས། །
NYAMPÉ NGÉSHÉ TING TSUK KYEWAR NGÉ
A deep and firm conviction will surely arise.

དེ་དུས་ལྟ་བའི་དེས་ཤེས་རྙེད་པ་ཡིན། །
DÉ DÜ TAWÉ NGÉSHÉ NYEPA YIN
At that time, you have found the conviction of the view.

འཛིན་པས་མ་བསླད་འཛིན་མེད་ངང་ལ་གློད། །
DZINPÉ MASLÉ DZINMÉ NGANG LA LÖ
Do not contaminate it with grasping, unleash in the state of non-fixation.

ངོ་སྤྲོད་ཐེབས་ནས་ཉམས་སུ་མ་ལོན་ཀྱང་། །
NGÖTRO THEB NÉ NYAM SU MALÖN KYANG
Once you got the introduction, even if you haven't fully integrated into your experience,

འཆི་ཚེ་བར་དོར་འཇིགས་སྐྲག་ཅི་བྱུང་ཡང་། །
CHI TSÉ BARDOR JIK TRAK CHI JUNG YANG
Whatever fear and terror arise at the time of death or in the bardo,

ཐམས་ཅད་རང་སྣང་སྟོང་པའི་རང་གཟུགས་སུ། །
TAMCHÉ RANGNANG TONGPÉ RANGZUK SU
Knowing all of them as your own empty appearances,

ཤེས་ནས་ཀ་དག་གཞི་ལ་འཚང་རྒྱ་འོ། །
SHÉ NÉ KADAK ZHI LA TSANG GYA O
You will attain enlightenment in the original purity.

ངོ་སྤྲོད་མ་ཐེབས་ཉམས་སུ་ལེན་པ་དེ། །
NGÖTRO MATHÉB NYAM SU LENPA DÉ
Putting this into practice without personally experiencing the direct introduction,

Song 16 - One Taste

དཔེར་ན་ཚེས་པ་གཅིག་ནས་འཆུགས་པ་ན། །
PER NA TSÉPA CHIK NÉ CHYUKPA NA
For example, it is just like missing the first day of the lunar calendar,

བཅོ་ལྔའི་བར་དུ་འཆུག་པ་ཇི་བཞིན་ནོ། །
CHONGA'I BARDU CHYUKPA JIZHIN NO
You will then miss all the way until the fifteenth day.

ཀུན་རྫོབ་ཆོས་རྣམས་ཐམས་ཅད་བདེན་མེད་དུ། །
KÜNDZOB CHÖ NAM TAMCHÉ DENMÉ DU
Without realizing that all conventional dharmas (relative experiences) are without inherent existence,

མ་རྟོགས་སྟོང་ཉིད་རྟོགས་ཟེར་རྫུན་ཆེན་ཡིན། །
MATOK TONGNYI TOK ZER DZÜN CHEN YIN
Saying you realize emptiness (without understanding this) is a deep lie.

དེས་ན་དོ་སྟྲོད་འདི་བཞིན་དང་པོའི་དུས། །
DÉ NA NGÖTRO DIBZHIN DANGPÖ DÜ
Therefore, regarding these introductions, in the very beginning,

བླ་མའི་དྲུང་དུ་སྡོད་ལ་གནས་ལུགས་ཀྱི། །
LAMÉ DRUNG DU DÖ LA NELUK KYI
Stay in the presence of the guru, and on the nature of reality,

སྟེང་དུ་གཏན་ལ་ཕོབ་དང་གོལ་ས་མེད། །
TENG DU TEN LA PHOB DANG GÖLSA MÉ
Settle firmly upon this, and there will
be no going astray.

དེའི་ཕྱིར་སྐལ་ལྡན་བུ་རྣམས་སྙིང་ལ་ཆོངས།། །།
DÉ CHIR KALDEN BU NAM NYING LA CHONG
Therefore, fortunate ones, hold this in your hearts!

SONG 17

View, Meditation, Lifestyle, & Result

ཧཱུྃ ཨེ་མ་ཧོ། ད་ཡང་སྐལ་ལྡན་རིགས་ཀྱི་བུ་རྣམས་ཉོན། །
EMAHO DA YANG KALDEN RIK KYI BU NAM NYÖN
Emaho! Now again, you of noble lineage who has good fortune, listen!

དེ་ལྟར་ལྟ་བའི་གནས་ལུགས་ཁོང་ཆུད་ནས། །
DETAR TAWÉ NELUK KHONG CHÜ NÉ
Having surely understood the nature of the view in that way,

འཁོར་ཡུལ་ཆགས་སྡང་འབྲེལ་ཐག་བད་ཀྱིས་ཆོད། །
KHOR YÜL CHAKDANG DRETHAK BÉ KYI CHÖ
Completely cut the thread of toxic attachment and aversion to the objects of samsara.

གཅིག་པུར་ནགས་ཀྱི་གསེབ་དང་རི་སུལ་དུ། །
CHIK PUR NAK KYI SEB DANG RI SUL DU
Alone, in the middle of forests and mountain valleys,

ལུས་ཀྱི་བྱ་རྩོལ་བོར་ནས་ལ་རྣལ་མར་སྡོད། །
LÜ KYI JATSÖL THONG LA NALMAR DÖ
Drop all physical works and stay in the natural state.

དག་གིས་སྨྲ་བརྗོད་ཆོད་ལ་བརྗོད་མེད་གྱིས། །
NGAK GI MAJÖ CHÖ LA JÖMÉ GYI
Drop all your speeches and stay silent,

སེམས་ནི་ནམ་མཁའ་བསམ་པའི་ཡུལ་ལས་འདས། །
SEM NI NAMKHA SAMPÉ YÜL LÉ DÉ
Mind is like space, beyond the realm of imagination.

དེ་ཡི་ངང་ལ་བཏང་བཞག་མེད་པར་གློད། །
DÉ YI NGANG LA TANG SHYAK MEPAR LÖ
In that state, relax without holding or placing.

སེམས་ལ་གཏད་སོ་མེད་ན་ལྟ་བ་ཡིན། །
SEM LA TEDSO MÉ NA TAWA YIN
When there is no point of reference in mind, that is the view.

བསྒོམ་དུ་མེད་པའི་ངང་ལ་གནས་པར་གྱིས། །
GOM DU MEPÉ NGANG LA NÉPAR GYI
Stay in the state where there is nothing to meditate on.

ཐོབ་མེད་རྫོགས་ཆེན་འབྲས་བུ་ཐོབ་པར་མཛོད། །
THOBMÉ DZOGCHEN DREBU THOBPAR DZÖ
Let the Dzogchen fruit (result), which is without achieving anything, be achieved.

དེ་ཡང་ལྟ་བར་མཉམ་པར་འཇོག་པའི་ཚེ། །
DÉ YANG TAWAR NYAMPAR JOKPÉ TSÉ
Also, when you meditate on the view,

འདི་ལྟར་རིག་པའི་ངང་ལ་འཇོག་སྙམ་དང་། །
DITAR RIGPÉ NGANG LA JOK NYAM DANG
Thinking, "I'm meditating in the state of awareness like this,"

Song 17 - View, Meditation, Lifestyle, & Result

ཕྱིང་ཆོད་དབང་དུ་ཤོར་འགྲོ་སྙམ་བྱེད་ཀྱི། །
YING GÖD WANG DU SHOR DRO NYAM JÉ KYI
Or thinking, "I am out of control," "Too many wild thoughts," or "Sinking into sleepiness",

རྟོག་པའི་དྲ་བ་གང་གིས་མི་བཅིངས་པར། །
TOKPÉ DRAWA GANG GI MI CHINGPAR
Without being bound by any web of such thoughts,

དམིགས་གཏད་ཆོས་མེད་ཧར་སང་རྒྱ་ཡན་ངང་། །
MIKTED CHÖMÉ HARSANG GYAYEN NGANG
In a state of aimless, unconfined, wide-open freedom,

ཟང་ཐལ་ཁ་ཡན་ཉིད་དུ་གློད་ལ་ཞོག །
ZANGTHAL KHAYEN NYI DU LÖ LA SHOK
Release and rest in a state of lucidity.

བློ་ཡི་ཆོས་ཀྱིས་བློ་འདས་དོན་མི་མཐོང་། །
LO YI CHÖ KYI LODÉ DÖN MI THONG
With the things of the intellect, you will not see the meaning beyond intellect.

བྱས་པའི་ཆོས་ཀྱིས་བྱར་མེད་སར་མི་སླེབ། །
JÉ PÉ CHÖ KYI CHARMÉ SAR MI LEB
With fabricated things (dharmas), you will not arrive at the place of no fabrication.

བློ་འདས་བྱར་མེད་དོན་དེ་ཐོབ་འདོད་ན། །
LODÉ CHARMÉ DÖN DÉ THOB DÖ NA
If you want to obtain that meaning beyond intellect and fabrication,

བཅོས་བསླད་མ་བྱེད་རིག་པ་གཅེར་བུར་ཞོག །
CHÖ LÉ MA JÉ RIKPA CHER BUR SHOK
Do not modify, leave awareness naked.

གཟུང་འཛིན་ཀུན་བྲལ་ལྟ་བའི་མཆོག་ཡིན་ནོ། །
ZUNGDZIN KÜNDRAL TAWÉ CHOK YIN NO
Being completely free from both projector and projection is the supreme view.

སྤང་བླང་མེད་པ་སྒོམ་པའི་མཆོག་ཡིན་ནོ། །
PANG LANG MÉPA GOMPÉ CHOK YIN NO
Remaining without accepting and avoiding is the supreme meditation.

བྱ་རྩོལ་ལས་འདས་སྤྱོད་པའི་མཆོག་ཡིན་ནོ། །
JATSÖL LÉ DÉ CHÖPÉ CHOK YIN NO
Resting beyond effort and activity is the supreme lifestyle.

རེ་མེད་རང་གནས་འབྲས་བུའི་མཆོག་ཡིན་ནོ། །
REMÉ RANGNÉ DREBÜ CHOK YIN NO
The naturally abiding state, free from hope and expectation, is the supreme result.

བལྟས་པས་མི་མཐོང་ལྟ་བའི་འཚོལ་འདྲོ་ཞོག །
TÉ PÉ MI THONG TAWÉ TSÖLTHRO SHOK
Since it cannot be seen by looking, give up searching for the view.

བསྒོམས་པས་མི་རྙེད་དྲན་འཛིན་དམིགས་གཏད་དོར། །
GOMPÉ MI NYÉ DREN DZIN MIKTED DOR
Since it cannot be found by meditating, abandon forced mindfulness, visualization and concentration,

Song 17 - View, Meditation, Lifestyle, & Result

སྤྱོད་པས་མི་འགྲུབ་སྒྱུ་མར་འཛིན་པ་ཐོངས། །
CHÖPÉ MI DRUB GYUMAR DZINPA THONG
Since it cannot be accomplished by any action, let go of holding on illusory things.

བཙལ་བས་མི་རྙེད་འབྲས་བུའི་རེ་བ་བོར། །
TSALWÉ MI NYÉ DREBÜ REWA BOR
Since it cannot be found by searching, let go of hope for a result.

ད་ལྟའི་ཤེས་པ་བཟོ་མེད་ལྷུག་པ་ལ། །
DA TI SHÉPA ZOMMÉ LHUKPA LA
In this present knowing, which is unfabricated and relaxed,

ཕྱོགས་རིས་མ་བྱེད་འཛིན་པས་མ་བསླད་ཅིག །
CHOK RI MA JÉ DZINPÉ MA LÉ CHIK
Do not be biased, do not contaminate it with grasping.

ད་ལྟའི་རིག་པ་དངོས་མེད་གསལ་བ་འདི། །
DA TI RIGPA NGO MÉ SALWA DI
This present awareness, which is clear and without substance,

འདི་ག་ལྟ་བ་ཀུན་གྱི་ཡང་རྩེ་ཡིན། །
DIGA TAWA KÜN GYI YANG TSÉ YIN
This itself is the very peak of all views.

དམིགས་གཏད་ཁྱབ་གདལ་བློ་དང་བྲལ་བ་འདི། །
MIKTED KHYABDAL LO DANG DRALWA DI
This aimless, vast, and beyond-intellect state,

འདི་ག་སྒོམ་པ་ཀུན་གྱི་ཡང་རྩེ་ཡིན། །
DIGA GOMPA KÜN GYI YANGTSÉ YIN
This itself is the very peak of all meditations.

ཨ་བཅོས་འཛིན་མེད་ལྷུག་པར་བཞག་པ་འདི། །
MACHÖ DZINMÉ LHUKPAR SHYAKPA DI
This unmodified, non-grasping, relaxed abiding,

འདི་ག་སྤྱོད་པ་ཀུན་གྱི་ཡང་རྩེ་ཡིན། །
DIGA CHÖPA KÜN GYI YANGTSÉ YIN
This itself is the very peak of all lifestyles.

མ་བཙལ་ཡེ་ནས་ལྷུན་གྱིས་གྲུབ་པ་འདི། །
MATSAL YENÉ LHÜN GYI DRUBPA DI
This which is spontaneously accomplished from the beginning, without seeking it,

འདི་ག་འབྲས་བུ་ཀུན་གྱི་ཡང་རྩེ་ཡིན། །
DIGA DREBU KÜN GYI YANGTSÉ YIN
This itself is the very peak of all results.

ལྟ་བའི་སྙིང་པོ་སྟོང་གསལ་འཛིན་མེད་ལྟོས། །
TAWÉ NYINGPO TONGSAL DZINMÉ TÖ
Look at the essence of the view: emptiness and clarity, without grasping.

སྒོམ་པའི་སྙིང་པོ་རང་གྲོལ་འཛིན་མེད་སྐྱོངས། །
GOMPÉ NYINGPO RANGDROL DZINMÉ KYONG
Maintain the essence of meditation: self-liberation, without fixation.

སྤྱོད་པའི་སྙིང་པོ་ཚོགས་དྲུག་ལྷུག་པར་ཤོག །
CHÖPÉ NYINGPO TSOK DRUK LHUKPAR SHOK
Rest in the essence of the lifestyle: free from engaging the six sensorial experiences.

Song 17 - View, Meditation, Lifestyle, & Result

འབྲས་བུའི་སྙིང་པོ་རེ་དོགས་ཞིག་པ་ཡིན། །
DREBÜ NYINGPO REDOK ZHIKPA YIN
Know the essence of the result: the end of hope and fear.

མུ་མཐའ་བྲལ་ན་ལྟ་བའི་རྒྱལ་པོ་མཆོག །
MÜTHA DRAL NA TAWÉ GYALPO CHOK
If it is without limit, it is the supreme king of views.

གཟེན་གཏད་བྲལ་ན་སྒོམ་པའི་རྒྱལ་པོ་མཆོག །
ZATÉ DRAL NA GOMPÉ GYALPO CHOK
If it is free from fixation, it is the supreme king of meditations.

བླང་དོར་བྲལ་ན་སྤྱོད་པའི་རྒྱལ་པོ་མཆོག །
LANGDOR DRAL NA CHÖPÉ GYALPO CHOK
If it is free from accepting and rejecting, it is the supreme king of lifestyles.

རེ་དོགས་བྲལ་ན་འབྲས་བུའི་རྒྱལ་པོ་མཆོག །
REDOK DRAL NA DREBÜ GYALPO CHOK
If it is free from hope and fear, it is the supreme king of results.

བལྟ་རུ་མེད་ཀྱིས་ལྟ་བའི་དམིགས་གཏད་དོར། །
TARU MÉ KYI TAWÉ MIKTED DOR
Since there is nothing to see, abandon the aim of the view.

བསྒོམ་དུ་མེད་ཀྱིས་གང་བྱུང་གང་བདེར་ཐོངས། །
GOM DU MÉ KYI GANG JUNG GANG DER THONG
Since there is nothing to meditate on, release whatever arises, in whatever way is comfortable.

སྤྱད་དུ་མེད་ཀྱིས་དགག་སྒྲུབ་སྤང་བླང་ཁྲོལ། །
CHÉ DU MÉ KYI GAKDRUB PANGLANG TROL
Since there is nothing to practice, be free from affirming and denying, abandoning and adopting.

འཐོབ་རྒྱུ་མེད་ཀྱིས་འབྲས་བུའི་རེ་བ་བོར། །
THOB GYU MÉ KYI DREBÜ REWA BOR
Since there is nothing to achieve, abandon hope for a result.

གང་ཡིན་ཡིན་གྱིས་ཆེད་འཛིན་མ་བྱེད་ཅིག །
GANG YIN YIN GYI CHÉ DZIN MAJÉ CHIK
Whatever it is, do not conceptually grasp at it — "It is this!"

འདི་ཡིན་མེད་ཀྱིས་དགག་སྒྲུབ་མ་བྱེད་ཅིག །
DI YIN MÉ KYI GAKDRUB MAJÉ CHIK
or "No, not this!" — Do not affirm or deny.

གཟའ་གཏད་མེད་ཀྱིས་ཕྱོགས་རིས་མ་བྱེད་ཅིག །
ZATÉ MÉ KYI CHOK RI MA JÉ CHIK
Since there is no fixation, do not be one-sided.

གདོད་ནས་དག་པའི་རང་རིག་རང་གསལ་ལ། །
DÖNÉ DAKPÉ RANGRIK RANGSAL LA
In self-knowing, self-clear awareness that is pure from the beginning,

བསམ་ཡུལ་བློ་ལས་འདས་པས་ལྟ་རུ་མེད། །
SAM YÜL LO LÉ DÉPÉ TARU MÉ
Beyond imagination and intellect, there is nothing to see.

Song 17 - View, Meditation, Lifestyle, & Result

དོ་བོ་གཞི་ནས་བྲལ་བས་བསྒོམ་དུ་མེད། །
NGOWO ZHI NÉ DRALWÉ GOM DU MÉ
Since its essence is free from any basis, there is nothing to meditate on.

རང་གྲོལ་མཐའ་ལས་འདས་པས་སྤྱད་དུ་མེད། །
RANGDROL THA LÉ DÉPÉ CHÉ DU MÉ
Since self-liberation is beyond any limit, there is nothing to practice.

རྩོལ་སྒྲུབ་ཞེན་པ་ལས་འདས་འབྲས་བུ་མེད། །
TSOL DRUB SHENPA LÉ DÉ DREBU MÉ
Since it is beyond attachment to effort and accomplishment, there is no result to seek.

དོ་བོ་སྟོང་ཉིད་ཡིན་པས་སྤང་ཐོབ་མེད། །
NGOWO TONGNYI YIN PÉ PANGTHOB MÉ
Since its essence is emptiness, there is no abandoning or obtaining.

རང་བཞིན་གསལ་སྟོང་ཡིན་པས་རྩོལ་སྒྲུབ་ཞིག །
RANGSHIN SAL TONG YIN PÉ TSOL DRUB SHYIK
Since its nature is clear and empty, cease effort and accomplishment.

ཐམས་ཅད་འགགས་མེད་ཡིན་པས་ཕྱོགས་རིས་མེད། །
TAMCHÉ GAKMÉ YIN PÉ CHOKRI MÉ
Since all is unceasing, there is no partiality.

གང་ལྟར་ཤར་ཡང་དེ་ལྟར་མ་འཛིན་ཅིག །
GANGTAR SHAR YANG DETAR MA DZIN CHIK
However it arises, do not grasp it in that way.

The Flight of Garuda

རྣལ་འབྱོར་ཤེས་པ་ནམ་མཁའི་བྱ་ལམ་འདྲ། །
NALJOR SHÉPA NAMKHÉ JA LAM DRA
The yogi's awareness is like the path of a bird in the sky.

བྱ་རྗེས་སྔ་མ་འགག་ནས་མི་མཐོང་ལྟར། །
JA JÉ NGAMA GAK NÉ MI THONG TAR
Just as the bird track ceases and is not seen,

དྲན་བསམ་སྔ་མ་འགག་ཅིང་མཐོང་བ་མེད། །
DREN SAM NGAMA GAK CHING THONGWA MÉ
Past thoughts and memories cease and are not seen.

དེ་ལ་རྗེས་བསྙེགས་འཛིན་པས་མ་མཐུད་ཅིག །
DÉ LA JÉNYEK DZINPÉ MA THÜ CHIK
Do not prolong them by chasing and grasping them (mental rumination).

བྱ་རྗེས་ཕྱི་མ་མ་འོངས་དངོས་མེད་ལྟར། །
JA JÉ CHIMA MA ONG NGOMÉ TAR
Just like the future bird track, which is not yet real,

དྲན་བསམ་ཕྱི་མས་བསུ་མ་མ་བྱེད་ཅིག །
DRENSAM CHIMÉ SUMA MAJÉ CHIK
Do not invite future thoughts and ideas.

བྱ་རྗེས་ད་ལྟ་ཁ་དོག་དབྱིབས་མེད་ལྟར། །
JA JÉ DA TA KHADOK YIBMÉ TAR
Just like the present bird track, which has no color or shape,

ད་ལྟའི་དྲན་བསམ་ཐ་མལ་རང་འགྲོས་ལ། །
DA TI DREN SAM THAMAL RANGDRÖ LA
In the ordinary, natural flow of present thoughts and feelings,

Song 17 - View, Meditation, Lifestyle, & Result

འདི་ཞེས་གཉེན་པོས་བཅོས་བསླད་མ་བྱེད་ཅིག །

DI SHÉ NYENPÖ CHÖ LÉ MAJÉ CHIK

Do not conceptually contaminate by thinking "This is it."

ཇི་ལྟར་ཤར་ཡང་དེ་ལྟར་མ་འཛིན་ཅིག །

JITAR SHAR YANG DETAR MA DZIN CHIK

However it may manifest, do not grasp it that way.

འདི་ནི་མཐར་ཐུག་སྙིང་པོའི་ལམ་འཁྱེར་ཡིན། །

DI NI THARTHUK NYINGPÖ LAM KHYER YIN

This is the ultimate, essential daily practice.

གང་ལྟར་ཤར་ཡང་དེ་ལྟར་མ་བཟུང་ན། །

GANGTAR SHAR YANG DETAR MA ZUNG NA

If you do not grasp whatever arises as being that way,

ཉོན་མོངས་རང་ཡལ་ཡེ་ཤེས་ཆེན་པོ་ཡིན། །

NYÖNMONG RANGYAL YESHE CHENPO YIN

The afflictions will naturally vanish, and reveal great wisdom.

སྐྱེ་མེད་བསམ་འདས་ཡེ་གྲོལ་ལྟ་བ་སྟེ། །

KYEMÉ SAMDÉ YEDROL TAWA TÉ

The view is unborn, beyond thought, and primordially liberated –

ནན་ཏན་བྱས་ན་བལྟ་རྒྱུ་མེད་པ་ལགས། །

NANTEN JÉ NA TAGYU MÉPA LAK

Concretely, there is nothing to see.

རང་བབས་ལྷོད་ཆགས་རང་གནས་སྒོམ་པ་སྟེ། །

RANGBAB LHÓCHAK RANGNÉ GOMPA TÉ

Meditation is naturally relaxed and self-abiding –

The Flight of Garuda

ནན་ཏན་བྱས་ན་བསྒོམ་རྒྱུ་མེད་པ་ལགས། །
NANTEN JÉ NA GOMGYU MÉPA LAK
Concretely, there is nothing to meditate on.

སྤང་བླང་གཉིས་མེད་སྒྱུ་མའི་སྤྱོད་པ་སྟེ། །
PANGLANG NYIMÉ GYÜ MÉ CHÖPA TÉ
Lifestyle is like an illusion, free from the duality of abandoning and adopting –

ནན་ཏན་བྱས་ན་སྤྱད་རྒྱུ་མེད་པ་ལགས། །
NANTEN JÉ NA CHÉ GYU MÉPA LAK
Concretely, there is nothing to practice.

རེ་དོགས་གཉིས་མེད་འབྲས་བུའི་རང་བཞིན་ཏེ། །
REDOK NYIMÉ DREBÜ RANGSHIN TÉ
The nature of the result is without the duality of hope and fear –

ནན་ཏན་བྱས་ན་འབྲས་བུ་མེད་པ་ལགས། །
NANTEN JÉ NA DREBU MÉPA LAK
Concretely, there is no result to obtain.

དུས་གསུམ་རྩ་བ་བྲལ་བའི་སེམས་ཉིད་འདི། །
DÜ SUM TSAWA DRALWÉ SEMNYI DI
This very nature of mind is without a root in the three times.

མ་བསྒོམ་མངོན་སུམ་སྣང་བ་བློ་རེ་བདེ། །
MAGOM NGÖNSUM NANGWA LO RÉ DE
Without meditating, staying with direct appearance,
mind is truly at ease.

Song 17 - View, Meditation, Lifestyle, & Result

ཐོག་མ་ཐ་མ་རང་བཞིན་དག་པའི་ཆོས། །
THOKMA THAMA RANGSHIN DAKPÉ CHÖ
The real nature, pure in its essence from beginning to end,

ཡེ་གྲོལ་ཡོངས་གྲོལ་འབད་རྩོལ་ཞིག་པ་མཚར། །
YEDROL YONGDROL BÉTSÖL ZHIKPA TSAR
Primordially liberated, completely liberated, effort has been broken! Amazing!

ཐ་མལ་ཤེས་པ་བཟོ་མེད་ལྷུག་པ་འདི། །
THAMAL SHÉPA ZOMMÉ LHUKPA DI
This ordinary knowing, unfabricated and relaxed,

རྒྱལ་བའི་དགོངས་པ་མཐའ་བྲལ་ཀློང་ཡངས་ཡིན། །
GYALWÉ GONGPA THADRAL LONG YANGS YIN
is the Buddha's intent, boundless and vast.

དེ་ཡང་འབད་པས་དཔྱད་ཅིང་བསྒོམས་པ་ཡིས། །
DÉ YANG BÉ PÉ PÉ CHING GOMPÉ YI
Even by diligently analyzing and meditating,

སེམས་ཉིད་གནས་ལུགས་གཉུག་མ་མཐོང་མི་འགྱུར། །
SEMNYI NELUK NYUKMA THONG MI GYUR
You will not see the true, inherent nature of mind.

མ་བསམས་མ་དཔྱད་ཐ་མལ་ཆོས་ཉིད་ལ། །
MASAM MAPÉ THARMAL CHÖNYI LA
In the basic nature of reality, without thinking or analyzing,

The Flight of Garuda

བསྒོམས་དང་མི་བསྒོམ་ཡེངས་དང་མ་ཡེངས་མེད། །
GOM DANG MIGOM YENG DANG MAYENG MÉ
There is no meditating or not meditating, no distraction or non-distraction.

མ་བསྒོམ་ལྷུག་པས་མང་པོ་གྲོལ་བ་ཡིན། །
MAGOM LHUKPÉ MANGPO DROLWA YIN
Though by this relaxed non-meditation, many have been naturally liberated.

གྲོལ་དང་མ་གྲོལ་དོན་ལ་གཉིས་སུ་མེད། །
DROL DANG MADROL DÖN LA NYISU MÉ
Liberation and non-liberation are not two in essence.

གནས་ལུགས་ཤེས་ན་རྩོལ་མེད་བློ་བདེ་འོ། །
NELUK SHÉ NA TSÖLMÉ LO DÉ O
If you know the true nature, an effortless ease of mind will come.

རྟོག་མེད་འདོད་པའི་རྟོག་པས་བཅིངས་པ་ན། །
TOKMÉ DÖPÉ TOKPÉ CHINGPA NA
When you are bound by the thought of wanting to be without thought,

རྣམ་རྟོག་ལངས་ནས་ཕྱོགས་བཅུར་འགྲོ་བར་བརྩོན། །
NAMTOK LANG NÉ CHOK CHUR DROWAR TSÖN
Conceptual thoughts will arise and increase in all ten directions.

འགྲོ་འོང་མེད་པ་རིག་པའི་གཞི་ཐོག་ཏུ། །
DRO ONG MÉPA RIGPÉ ZHI THOK TU
In the nature of awareness, which has no coming or going,

Song 17 - View, Meditation, Lifestyle, & Result

ཁ་ཡན་གློད་ནས་རང་ཡན་བཞག་པ་ན། །
KHAYEN LÖ NÉ RANGYEN SHYAKPA NA
When you release openly and leave it as it is,

མི་གཡོ་རི་བོ་བཞིན་དུ་བརྟན་པར་གནས། །
MIYO RIWO ZHIN DU TENPAR NÉ
It will remain stable like an unmoving mountain.

གོ་ལྡོག་འགྲོས་འདི་བུ་རྣམས་ཤེས་པར་གྱིས། །
GODOK DRÖ DI BU NAM SHÉPAR GYI
Child, understand this paradoxical way of proceeding:

འདི་ལ་བསྒོམ་རྒྱུ་རྡུལ་ཙམ་མི་དམིགས་ཀྱང་། །
DI LA GOMGYU DULTSAM MI MIK KYANG
Although you do not find even a speck of something to meditate on in this,

ཡེངས་མེད་དྲན་པས་བཟིན་པ་རབ་ཏུ་གཅེས།། ༎
YENGMÉ DRENPÉ ZINPA RAB TU CHÉ
It is vital to keep undistracted mindfulness.

SONG 18

Beyond Meditation

ཨེ་མ་ཧོ། ད་ཡང་སྐལ་ལྡན་བུ་རྣམས་ཚུར་ཉོན་དང་། །
EMAHO DA YANG KALDEN BU NAM TSHUR NYÖN DANG
Emaho! Now again, fortunate ones, listen to me.

ཕྱི་ཡུལ་མེད་སྣང་སྟོང་པའི་རང་གཟུགས་འདི། །
CHI YÜL MÉ NANG TONGPÉ RANGZUK DI
Appearing outer objects are the self-dispay of emptiness,

ཡེ་སྟོང་ཆུ་ཟླ་འདྲ་བས་སྦྱང་མི་དགོས། །
YETONG CHUZLA DRAWÉ JANG MI GÖ
Being primordially empty, like a reflection of the moon in water, there's no need for purification.

ནང་གི་དྲན་རྟོག་རང་ཡལ་རྗེས་མེད་པས། །
NANG GI DRENTOK RANGYAL JÉMÉ PÉ
Since inner thoughts and concepts naturally vanish without a trace,

འབད་རྩོལ་གཉེན་པོ་དེ་ལ་འཇུག་མི་དགོས། །
BÉTSÖL NYENPO DÉ LA JUK MI GÖ
You do not need to engage in effort or apply an antidote for them.

Song 18 - Beyond Meditation

སྣང་སེམས་ཡེ་གྲོལ་ལྷུག་པའི་ཡེ་ཤེས་ལ། །
NANGSEM YEDROL LHUKPÉ YESHE LA
In the primordially liberated, relaxed wisdom of manifestation and mind,

སྤང་བླང་རེ་དོགས་གང་གིའང་སྒྱུ་མི་འདོགས། །
PANGLANG REDOK GANG GI'ANG DRO MI DOK
Do not fake with any accepting, rejecting, hope, or fear, of any kind.

རིག་པ་ཟང་ཀ་གཅེར་བུ་འདི་ཉིད་ལ། །
RIGPA ZANGKA CHERBU DI NYI LA
In this naked, clear awareness,

ཡིད་དཔྱོད་སྤྲོས་པའི་གོན་པ་མ་བགོན་པར། །
YIDCHÖ TRÖPÉ GÖNPA MA KÖNPAR
Without putting on the clothes of intellectual elaboration,

ཤིག་སེ་ཁྲེས་སེ་བུན་ནེ་རྗེས་མེད་དུ། །
SHIK SÉ THRÉ SÉ BÜN NÉ JÉMÉ DU
Suddenly, spontaneously, leaving no sign,

རིས་མེད་མཉམ་པ་ཆེན་པོར་གློད་ལ་ཞོག །
RIMÉ NYAMPA CHENPOR LÖ LA SHOK
Chill out in the great equality, without any distinctions.

དེ་ཡི་ངང་ལ་དྲན་བསམ་ཅི་ཤར་ཡང་། །
DÉ YI NGANG LA DRENSAM CHI SHAR YANG
Whatever thoughts or memories arise in that state,

རིམེད་རང་བྱུང་རིག་པའི་རང་གདངས་སུ། །
RIMÉ RANGJUNG RIGPÉ RANGDANG SU
Know them as the self-radiance of naturally arising, undistracted awareness.

ཤེས་པར་གྱིས་ལ་རྗེས་ནི་མི་སྙེགས་པར། །
SHÉPAR GYI LA JÉ NI MI NYEKPAR
Know this and do not chase after them.

སྣང་སེམས་ཁྲལ་མ་ཁྲོལ་དང་སངས་མ་སངས། །
NANGSEM THRAL MATHROL DANG SANG MASANG
Appearances in mind, whether troubled or untroubled, awake or unclear,

འལ་མ་འོལ་གྱི་ཆོས་ཉིད་ཡོ་ལང་དུ། །
AL MA OL GYI CHÖNYI YOLANG DU
In the natural swing of reality, whether sure or not sure,

རྒྱ་ཕྱམ་ཉིད་དུ་བཏང་ན་ཀུན་བཟང་གི །
GYACHAM NYI DU TANG NA KÜNZANG GI
If you allow it to be in its own spaciousness,

དགོངས་པའི་ཀློང་དུ་ད་ལྟ་བསླེབས་པ་ཡིན། །
GONGPÉ LONG DU DA TA LEBPA YIN
Now you have reached the state of realization.

རྫོགས་པ་ཆེན་པོ་ཡེ་གྲོལ་ལྷུན་གྲུབ་ཀྱི། །
DZOGPA CHENPO YEDROL LHÜNDRUB KYI
This is called Dzogpa Chenpo - originally liberated and spontaneously accomplished,

Song 18 - Beyond Meditation

སྣ་ཚོགས་རང་གྲོལ་རྣལ་འབྱོར་དེ་ལ་ཟེར། །
NATSOK RANGDROL NALJOR DÉ LA ZER
Such a practitioner is known as a Natsok Rangdrol Yogin
(all self-liberated yogi or yogini)

མ་ཕྱིན་ན་ཡང་སངས་རྒྱས་ས་རུ་བསླེབས། །
MACHIN NA YANG SANG GYÉ SA RU LEB
Even without travelling, you have arrived at the state of Buddhahood.

མ་བསྒྲུབས་ན་ཡང་འབྲས་བུ་ལྷུན་གྱིས་གྲུབ། །
MADRUB NA YANG DREBU LHÜN GYI DRUB
Even without practicing, the result is spontaneously accomplished.

མ་སྤངས་བཞིན་དུ་ཉོན་མོངས་རང་སར་དག །
MAPANG ZHINDU NYÖNMONG RANGSAR DAK
Even without avoiding, the afflictions are purified in their own place.

བླ་མ་དམ་པའི་དགོངས་པ་དང་མཉམ་མོ། །
LAMA DAMPÉ GONGPA DANG NYAMMO
This is the same as the realization of the qualified gurus.

རྗེས་སུ་བསྙེགས་སོ་ལས་རྣམས་ཟིན་པ་འོ། །
JÉSU NYEK SO LÉ NAM ZINPA O
Become true followers and all spiritual work is done.

གནད་འདི་ཡིན་པས་བུ་རྣམས་ཤེས་པར་གྱིས། །
NED DI YIN PÉ BU NAM SHÉPAR GYI
This is the key point, so my kids, understand it!

ཕ་རྒན་ཆོས་ཀྱི་རྒྱལ་པོའི་བཀའ་དྲིན་གྱིས། །
PHAGEN CHÖKYI GYALPÖ KADRIN GYI
Through the kindness of the wise father, the King of Dharma (Chogyal Ngawang Dargye)

བྱ་བྲལ་ལྷུན་གྱིས་གྲུབ་པའི་དགོངས་པ་རུ། །
JA DRAL LHÜN GYI DRUBPÉ GONGPA RU
The effortless, spontaneously accomplished mind realm,

ཚོགས་དྲུག་རང་གྲོལ་ད་རེས་བསླེབས་པ་འོ། །
TSOK DRUK RANGDROL DARÉ LEBPA O
Has now been reached by Tsokdruk Rangdrol.

གནད་འདི་ཡིན་ཀྱང་ལ་ལས་མ་གོ་འདུག །
NED DI YIN KYANG LA LÉ MAGO DUK
Although this is the key point, many have not understood it.

ཐམས་ཅད་ཡེ་ཟིན་འདུག་སྟེ་ཡང་བྱེད་དོ། །
TAMCHÉ YÉ ZIN DUK TÉ YANG JÉ DO
Everything is primordially complete, yet still they act;

ཡེ་གྲོལ་ཉིད་དུ་འདུག་སྟེ་ཡང་དགྲོལ་ལོ། །
YEDROL NYI DU DUK TÉ YANG DROL LO
It is primordially liberated, yet still they try to liberate it;

ཡེ་བཞག་ཉིད་དུ་འདུག་སྟེ་ཡང་འཇོག་གོ །
YESHYAK NYI DU DUK TÉ YANG JOK GO
It is primordially resting, yet still they try to make it rest;

ཡེ་བསྒོམས་ཉིད་དུ་འདུག་སྟེ་ཡང་བསྒོམ་མོ། །
YEGOM NYI DU DUK TÉ YANG GOM MO
Primordially meditating, yet still they try to meditate;

Song 18 - Beyond Meditation

ཡེ་བལྟས་ཉིད་དུ་འདུག་སྟེ་ཡང་བལྟ་འོ། །
YETÉ NYI DU DUK TÉ YANG TA O
Primordially seeing, yet still they try to see;

ཡེ་བགྲོད་ཉིད་དུ་འདུག་སྟེ་ཡང་བགྲོད་དོ། །
YEDRÖ NYI DU DUK TÉ YANG DRÖ DO
Primordially gone, yet they still want to go somewhere —

ཟེར་ནས་ཡིད་དཔྱོད་ལྟ་བར་རེ་བའི་མིས། །
ZER NÉ YIDCHÖ TAWAR RE WÉ MI
Saying this, people hoping for the view through intellectual analysis,

ཐོས་ཀྱང་ཚིག་རོ་གོ་ཡང་རྣམ་རྟོག་གོ །
THÖ KYANG TSIKRO GO YANG NAMTOK GO
Even if they hear, it's just words; even if they understand, it's just concepts;

རྟོགས་ཀྱང་ཕོ་ཚོད་བསྒོམས་ཀྱང་བློས་བྱས་སོ། །
TOK KYANG PHOTSHÖ GOM KYANG LÖ JÉ SO
Even if they think they realize, it's just an intellectual understanding; even if they meditate, it's fabricated by the mind.

དཔྱད་ཀྱང་གཉིས་འཛིན་བསྒྲུབས་ཀྱང་འཁོར་བ་འོ། །
PÉ KYANG NYIDZIN DRUB KYANG KHORWA O
Even if they analyze, it's based on dualistic grasping; even if they practice, it leads to samsara.

ཆོས་ཉིད་ཡིད་དཔྱོད་མཁན་གྱི་མི་དེ་ལ། །
CHÖNYI YIDCHÖ KHEN GYI MI DÉ LA
For that person who intellectually analyzes the nature of reality,

The Flight of Garuda

རྫོགས་ཆེན་སྙིང་ཐིག་ལས་འབྲེལ་མེད་པར་ངེས། །
DZOGCHEN NYINGTHIK LÉ DRELMÉ PAR NGÉ
Know for certain that they have no connection to the heart essence of Dzogchen.

བྱ་བྱེད་མི་དགོས་བྱས་པས་ཟིན་པ་མེད། །
JAJÉ MI GÖ JÉ PÉ ZINPA MÉ
You don't need to do many things; it is not grasped by doing.

བྱ་དང་མི་བྱའི་རྩིས་ལས་འདས་པ་འོ། །
JA DANG MIJÉ TSI LÉ DÉPA O
It is beyond the calculations of doing and not doing.

བསྒོམ་མེད་སྒོམ་པ་ལས་འདས་བསྒོམས་ཀྱང་འཕུང་། །
GOMMÉ GOMPA LÉ DÉ GOM KYANG PHUNG
There is no meditation (it's beyond), if you meditate, you will fail.

བལྟར་མེད་ལྟ་བ་ལས་འདས་གང་ལ་བལྟ། །
TAR MÉ TAWA LÉ DÉ GANG LA TA
There is no view (it's beyond views), so what are you looking at?

བཙལ་མེད་བཙལ་བ་ལས་འདས་རྙེད་པ་མེད། །
TSALMÉ TSALWA LÉ DÉ NYEPA MÉ
There is no need to search (it's beyond searching), there is nothing to find.

འདི་ལྟར་རིག་པ་ཟང་མ་ཐལ་བྱུང་དུ། །
DITAR RIGPA ZANG MA THAL JUNG DU
In this way, although awareness is translucent,

Song 18 - Beyond Meditation

འདུག་སྟེ་བཤད་ཀྱང་མི་ཉན་མི་དེ་ལ། །
DUK TÉ SHÉ KYANG MI NYEN MI DÉ LA
Even if it is present and explained, that person does not listen,

རྫོགས་ཆེན་ལས་འབྲེལ་མེད་པ་དགོད་རེ་བྲོ། །
DZOGCHEN LÉ DRELMÉ PA GÖ RÉ DRO
It is almost laughable that they have no connection to Dzogchen.

གང་ལ་བལྟས་ཀྱང་ཀ་དག་ཀློང་ཆེན་གྱི། །
GANG LA TÉ KYANG KADAK LONGCHEN GYI
Whatever you look at, it arises as the realization of the great expanse of original purity.

དགོངས་པར་ཤར་བས་འཁོར་འདས་གཉིས་སུ་མེད། །
GONGPAR SHARWÉ KHORDÉ NYISU MÉ
Because it arises as realization, samsara and nirvana are not two.

དེ་འདྲའི་དགོངས་པ་གླུ་རུ་བླངས་པ་ལ། །
DI DRA'I GONGPA LU RU LANGPA LA
When such realization is sung as a song,

དུས་གསུམ་རྒྱལ་བ་དགྱེས་པར་གདོན་མི་ཟ། །
DÜ SUM GYALWA GYEPAR DÖN MI ZA
The Buddhas of the three times will undoubtedly be pleased.

འོ་ན་ཕྱི་རོལ་འཁྲུལ་པའི་སྣང་ཡུལ་དུ། །
O NA CHIROL THRULPÉ NANGYÜL DU
Then, in the outer field of illusory appearances,

རང་སར་ཡན་དུ་བཅུག་ན་སླར་ལ་ཡང་། །
RANGSAR YEN DU CHUK NA SLAR LA YANG
If you just leave it naturally as it is,

The Flight of Garuda

འཁྲུལ་པར་མི་འགྲོ་འམ་ཞེས་བརྗོད་གྱུར་ན། །
THRULPAR MI DRO AM ZHÉ JÖ GYUR NA
You might wonder, "Will it not again go into delusion?"

ཐ་མལ་མི་ཡིས་བདག་ཏུ་བཟུང་པས་འཁྲུལ། །
THARMAL MI YI DAKTU ZUNGPÉ THRUL
Ordinary people are deluded because they grasp at things as real.

རྣལ་འབྱོར་པ་ཡིས་གཞི་མེད་རྩ་བྲལ་དུ། །
NALJORPA YI ZHI MÉ TSA DRAL DU
Yogis and Yoginis, knowing it to be without basis or root,

ཤེས་པས་བཅོས་བསླད་བླང་དོར་མི་བྱེད་པར། །
SHÉPÉ CHÖ LÉ LANGDOR MIJÉ PAR
Without fabricating, modifying, accepting, or rejecting,

རང་བབ་འཛིན་མེད་བཞག་པས་མི་འཁྲུལ་ལོ། །
RANGBAB DZINMÉ SHYAKPÉ MI THRUL LO
By naturally resting without grasping, they will not be deluded.

འདི་ལ་གོལ་ས་ཇི་ཡོད་བརྗོད་གྱུར་ན། །
DI LA GÖLSA É YÖ JÖ GYUR NA
If you say, "Is there any dangerous side effect of this?"

འདི་ལ་གོལ་ས་ནོར་ས་གཅིག་ཀྱང་མེད། །
DI LA GÖLSA NORSA CHIK KYANG MÉ
In this, there is not even one side effect or risk.

གོལ་ས་ཞེན་ཅིང་ཆགས་ན་ཡོད་པ་ཡིན། །
GÖLSA SHEN CHING CHAK NA YÖPA YIN
Side effects exist if you cling and are attached.

Song 18 - Beyond Meditation

གང་ཤར་ཉིད་ལ་འཛིན་པ་མེད་པ་ན། །
GANG SHAR NYI LA DZINPA MÉPA NA
When there is no grasping at whatever arises,

གོལ་སར་ལྟུང་རྒྱུ་ཞིག་ནི་ག་ལ་འོངས། །
GOLSAR TUNG GYU SHYIK NI GALA ONG
How could there be any reason to fall into danger?

འོན་ཀྱང་རིག་པ་ཡུལ་ལ་འཆར་དུས་སུ། །
ÖN KYANG RIGPA YÜL LA CHAR DÜ SU
However, when awareness arises in relation to objects,

གང་ཤར་རྣམ་པར་རྟོག་པའི་ངོ་བོ་ལ། །
GANG SHAR NAMPAR TOKPÉ NGOWO LA
Whatever arises in the nature of conceptual thoughts,

ལྟ་བ་དེ་ཉིད་བསྒོམ་དུ་འདོད་པ་མིན། །
TAWA DÉ NYI GOM DU DÖPA MIN
Merely looking at that is not the basis of the meditation.

དེ་ཡི་དུས་ཀྱི་རིག་པ་ས་ལེ་བ། །
DÉ YI DÜ KYI RIGPA SALEWA
In that moment, when present awareness is vivid and fresh,

རྗེན་པའི་ཆ་དེ་ཕྱལ་ལེ་སྐྱོང་བ་འོ། །
JENPÉ CHA DÉ CHAL LÉ KYONGWA O
Maintain that naked aspect without obstruction.

དེ་ཡང་རིག་པ་འཕྲོ་འདུ་མེད་པ་རུ། །
DÉ YANG RIGPA THRO DU MÉPA RU
Also, in that pure knowing which has no coming or going,

གནས་པའི་དུས་ཀྱི་གནས་ཆའི་མི་རྟོག་པ། །
NÉ PÉ DÜ KYI NÉ CHÉ MITOKPA
Merely remaining in a thought-free state,

དེ་ཉིད་བསྒོམ་གྱི་དངོས་གཞི་མ་ཡིན་ཏེ། །
DÉ NYI GOM GYI NGOZHI MAYIN TÉ
That is not the actual basis of meditation.

དེ་ཡི་དུས་ཀྱི་ཧྲིག་གེ་སང་དེ་བའི། །
DÉ YI DÜ KYI HRIK GÉ SANG NGÉ BA'I
In that moment, bright, clear, and vivid,

གསལ་དྭངས་དར་ཆ་དེ་ཉིད་སྐྱོང་བ་འོ། །
SALDANG NGARCHA DÉ NYI KYONGWA O
Maintain that very clarity and sharpness.

གནད་འདི་མ་གོ་འཆར་གནས་གཉིས་ཀ་ལ། །
NED DI MAGO CHAR NÉ NYI KA LA
If you do not understand this key point and think that in both arising and abiding,

བལྟ་བ་དེ་ཉིད་སྒོམ་པའི་དོ་བོ་ཡིན། །
TAWA DÉ NYI GOMPÉ NGOWO YIN
Merely watching these occurrences is the essence of meditation,

སྙམ་ན་འཁྲུལ་པར་འགྱུར་རོ་སྙིང་གི་བུ། །
NYAM NA THRULPAR GYUR RO NYING GI BU
If you think that, you will be mistaken, heart child.

Song 18 - Beyond Meditation

གནས་པ་ཙམ་ནི་བསམ་གཏན་ལྷ་དང་འདྲ། །
NÉPA TSAM NI SAMTEN LHA DANG DRA
Simply abiding is like the samadhi of gods.

འཆར་བ་ཙམ་ནི་ཐ་མལ་རྟོག་པ་འདྲ། །
CHARWA TSAM NI THARMAL TOKPA DRA
Simply arising is like ordinary conceptual thought.

དེ་ལ་བསྒོམས་ཀྱང་སངས་རྒྱས་འཐོབ་མི་འགྱུར། །
DÉ LA GOM KYANG SANG GYÉ THOB MI GYUR
If you meditate on that, you will not attain Buddhahood.

མདོར་ན་གང་གི་དུས་སུའང་རིག་པའི་ཆ། །
DOR NA GANG GI DÜ SU'ANG RIGPÉ CHA
In short, at any time, the aspect of awareness,

རྗེན་པ་ཟང་ཐལ་ཤེལ་གོང་འདྲ་བ་དེ། །
JENPA ZANGTHAL SHEL GONG DRAWA DÉ
That is naked, clear, and transparent like a crystal ball.

ཀློང་དུ་མ་གྱུར་བར་དུ་ས་ལེར་སྐྱོངས། །
LONG DU MAGYUR WARDU SALER KYONG
Maintain it clearly until it becomes experiential.

གྱུར་ནས་དེ་ཡི་ངང་ལ་འབྲལ་མེད་གྱིས། །
GYUR NÉ DÉ YI NGANG LA DRALMÉ GYI
Once it becomes fully encompassing, remain inseparable from that state.

ཁྲེགས་ཆོད་ལྟ་བའི་གནད་འགག་རིག་པ་ནི། །
TREKCHÖ TAWÉ NEDGAK RIGPA NI
The key point of the Trekchö view is awareness.

The Flight of Garuda

ཇེན་ལ་ཕུད་ནས་ས་ལེར་སྐྱོང་བ་ལ། །
JEN LA PHÜ NÉ SALER KYONGWA LA
To leave it naked and maintain it clearly.

ཟེར་བས་གནད་འདི་ཁོ་ན་གལ་ཆེ་སྟེ། །
ZERWÉ NED DI KHONA GALCHÉ TÉ
This key point is very important.

འདི་ནི་ཚིག་བརྒྱའི་མདོ་འགག་ཡིན་པས་ན། །
DI NI TSIK GYÉ DOGAK YIN PÉ NA
Since it is the key point of a hundred words,

སྐལ་ལྡན་སྙིང་གི་བུ་རྣམས་ཤེས་པར་གྱིས།། །།
KALDEN NYING GI BU NAM SHÉPAR GYI
Fortunate heart child, understand this!

SONG 19

Present Awareness

ཨེ་མ་ཧོ། ད་ཡང་སེམས་ཀྱི་བུ་རྣམས་གུས་པས་ཉོན། །
EMAHO DA YANG SEM KYI BU NAM GÜPÉ NYÖN
Emaho! Now again, sons and daughters of mind, listen respectfully.

ནོར་ས་མེད་པའི་ཐིག་ཆེན་བཞི་བསྟན་པ། །
NORSA MEPÉ THIG CHEN ZHI TENPA
Now I shall reveal the four fine lines without error:

ལྟ་བ་ནོར་ས་མེད་པའི་ཐིག་ཆེན་ནི། །
TAWA NORSA MEPÉ THIG CHEN NI
The fine line of the view without error is:

ད་ལྟའི་ཤེས་པ་ས་ལེ་འདི་ཀ་ཡིན། །
DA TI SHÉPA SALÉ DI KA YIN
Directly present, clear awareness (now and here).

གསལ་ལ་མི་ནོར་བས་ན་ཐིག་ཅེས་བྱ། །
SAL LA MI NORWÉ NA THIG JÉ JA
Because it is clear and without error, it is called a fine line.

The Flight of Garuda

སྒོམ་པ་ནོར་ས་མེད་པའི་ཐིག་ཆེན་ནི། །
GOMPA NORSA MEPÉ THIG CHEN NI
The fine line of meditation without error is:

ད་ལྟའི་ཤེས་པ་ས་ལེ་འདི་ག་ཡིན། །
DA TI SHÉPA SALÉ DI KA YIN
Directly present, clear awareness (now and here).

གསལ་ལ་མི་ནོར་བས་ན་ཐིག་ཅེས་བྱ། །
SAL LA MI NORWÉ NA THIG JÉ JA
Because it is clear and without error, it is called a fine line.

སྤྱོད་པ་ནོར་ས་མེད་པའི་ཐིག་ཆེན་ནི། །
CHÖPA NORSA MEPÉ THIG CHEN NI
The fine line of lifestyle without error is:

ད་ལྟའི་ཤེས་པ་ས་ལེ་འདི་ག་ཡིན། །
DA TI SHÉPA SALÉ DI KA YIN
Directly present, clear awareness (now and here).

གསལ་ལ་མི་ནོར་བས་ན་ཐིག་ཅེས་བྱ། །
SAL LA MI NORWÉ NA THIG JÉ JA
Because it is clear and without error, it is called a fine line.

འབྲས་བུ་ནོར་ས་མེད་པའི་ཐིག་ཆེན་ནི། །
DREBU NORSA MEPÉ THIG CHEN NI
The fine line of the result without error is:

ད་ལྟའི་ཤེས་པ་ས་ལེ་འདི་ག་ཡིན། །
DA TI SHÉPA SALÉ DI KA YIN
Directly present, clear awareness (now and here).

Song 19 - Present Awareness

གསལ་ལ་མི་ནོར་བས་ན་ཐིག་ཅེས་བྱ། །
SAL LA MI NORWÉ NA THIG JÉ JA
Because it is clear and without error, it is called a fine line.

མི་འགྱུར་བ་ཡི་གཟེར་ཆེན་བཞི་བསྟན་པ། །
MIGYURWA YI ZER CHEN ZHI TENPA
Now I will reveal the four great unchanging nails.

ལྟ་བ་འགྱུར་བ་མེད་པའི་གཟེར་ཆེན་ནི། །
TAWA GYURWA MEPÉ ZER CHEN NI
The unchangeable great nail of the view is:

ད་ལྟའི་ཤེས་པ་ས་ལེ་འདི་ག་ཡིན། །
DA TI SHÉPA SALÉ DI KA YIN
Directly present, clear awareness (now and here).

དུས་གསུམ་བརྟན་པའི་ཕྱིར་ན་གཟེར་ཞེས་བྱ། །
DÜ SUM TENPÉ CHIR NA ZER ZHÉ JA
Because it is stable in the three times, it is called a nail.

སྒོམ་པ་འགྱུར་བ་མེད་པའི་གཟེར་ཆེན་ནི། །
GOMPA GYURWA MEPÉ ZER CHEN NI
The unchangeable great nail of the meditation is:

ད་ལྟའི་ཤེས་པ་ས་ལེ་འདི་ག་ཡིན། །
DA TI SHÉPA SALÉ DI KA YIN
Directly present, clear awareness (now and here).

དུས་གསུམ་བརྟན་པའི་ཕྱིར་ན་གཟེར་ཞེས་བྱ། །
DÜ SUM TENPÉ CHIR NA ZER ZHÉ JA
Because it is stable in the three times, it is called a nail.

སྤྱོད་པ་འགྱུར་བ་མེད་པའི་གཟེར་ཆེན་ནི། །
CHÖPA GYURWA MEPÉ ZER CHEN NI
The unchangeable great nail of the lifestyle is:

ད་ལྟའི་ཤེས་པ་ས་ལེ་འདི་ག་ཡིན། །
DA TI SHÉPA SALÉ DI KA YIN
Directly present, clear awareness (now and here).

དུས་གསུམ་བརྟན་པའི་ཕྱིར་ན་གཟེར་ཞེས་བྱ། །
DÜ SUM TENPÉ CHIR NA ZER ZHÉ JA
Because it is stable in the three times, it is called a nail.

འབྲས་བུ་འགྱུར་བ་མེད་པའི་གཟེར་ཆེན་ནི། །
DREBU GYURWA MEPÉ ZER CHEN NI
The unchangeable great nail of the result is:

ད་ལྟའི་ཤེས་པ་ས་ལེ་འདི་ག་ཡིན། །
DA TI SHÉPA SALÉ DI KA YIN
Directly present, clear awareness (now and here).

དུས་གསུམ་བརྟན་པའི་ཕྱིར་ན་གཟེར་ཞེས་བྱ། །
DÜ SUM TENPÉ CHIR NA ZER ZHÉ JA
Because it is stable in the three times, it is called a nail.

ལྟ་བ་མི་མཐུན་རྒྱ་ཆེ་གྲངས་མང་ཡང་། །
TAWA MITHÜN GYACHÉ DRANG MANG YANG
Although there are many vast and numerous different views.

Song 19 - Present Awareness

དུ་ལྟའི་རང་རིག་རང་བྱུང་ཡེ་ཤེས་ལ། །
DA TI RANGRIK RANGJUNG YESHE LA
In this present self-knowing, self-arising wisdom.

བལྟ་བྱ་དང་ནི་ལྟ་བྱེད་གཉིས་སུ་མེད། །
TABJA DANG NI TAJÉ NYISU MÉ
There is no division between view and viewer.

ལྟ་བ་མ་བལྟ་ལྟ་བའི་མཁན་པོ་ཚོལ། །
TAWA MATA TAWÉ KHENPO TSÖL
Do not look at the view, search for the projector.

ལྟ་བའི་མཁན་པོ་བཙལ་བས་མ་རྙེད་ན། །
TAWÉ KHENPO TSALWÉ MANYÉ NA
If you search for the projector and do not find it,

དེའི་ཚེ་ལྟ་བ་ཟད་སར་འཁྱོལ་བ་ཡིན། །
DÉ TSÉ TAWA ZÉSAR KHYÖLWA YIN
At that time, the view is worn out.

ལྟ་བ་བལྟ་རྒྱུ་ཅི་ཡང་མེད་པ་ལ། །
TAWA TAGYU CHIYANG MÉPA LA
In the view where there is nothing whatsoever to see.

ཡེ་མེད་སྟོང་ཆད་ཧ་པོར་མ་སོང་བར། །
YEMÉ TONGCHÉ HAPOR MASONG WAR
Without going into a state of blank nothingness or emptiness.

ད་ལྟའི་ཤེས་པ་མ་བཅོས་ས་ལེ་བ། །
DA TI SHÉPA MACHÖ SALEWA
This present, unmodified, clear awareness,

The Flight of Garuda

རྫོགས་པ་ཆེན་པོའི་ལྟ་བ་དེ་ག་ཡིན། །
DZOGPA CHENPÖ TAWA DÉ GA YIN
That itself is the view of Dzogpa Chenpo (Ati Yoga).

སྒོམ་པ་མི་མཐུན་རྒྱ་ཆེ་གྲངས་མང་ཡང་། །
GOMPA MITHÜN GYACHÉ DRANG MANG YANG
Although there are many vast and numerous different meditations,

ད་ལྟའི་ཐ་མལ་ཤེས་པ་ཟང་ཐལ་ལ། །
DA TI THARMAL SHÉPA ZANGTHAL LA
In this present ordinary knowing, which is transparent and open,

བསྒོམ་བྱ་དང་ནི་སྒོམ་བྱེད་གཉིས་སུ་མེད། །
GOMJA DANG NI GOMJÉ NYISU MÉ
There is no division between meditation and meditator.

སྒོམ་པ་མ་སྒོམས་སྒོམ་པའི་མཁན་པོ་ཚོལ། །
GOMPA MAGOM GOMPÉ KHENPO TSÖL
Do not meditate on meditation, search for the meditator.

སྒོམ་པའི་མཁན་པོ་བཙལ་བས་མ་རྙེད་ན། །
GOMPÉ KHENPO TSALWÉ MANYÉ NA
If you search for the meditator and do not find her,

དེའི་ཚེ་སྒོམ་པ་ཟད་སར་འཁྱོལ་བ་ཡིན། །
DÉ TSÉ GOMPA ZÉSAR KHYÖLWA YIN
At that time, meditation is worn out.

སྒོམ་པ་བསྒོམ་རྒྱུ་ཅི་ཡང་མེད་པ་ལ། །
GOMPA GOMGYU CHIYANG MÉPA LA
In the meditation where there is nothing whatsoever to meditate on,

Song 19 - Present Awareness

བྱིང་རྒོད་འཐིབས་རྨུགས་དབང་དུ་མ་སོང་བར། །
JING GÖ THIB MUK WANG DU MASONG WAR
Without falling under the power of dullness, agitation, cloudiness, or sleepiness,

ད་ལྟའི་ཤེས་པ་མ་བཅོས་རང་གསལ་ལ། །
DA TI SHÉPA MACHÖ RANGSAL LA
This present awareness, unmodified, is self-clear.

མ་བཅོས་མཉམ་པར་འཇོག་པ་སྒོམ་པ་ཡིན། །
MACHÖ NYAMPAR JOKPA GOMPA YIN
To rest without modification is meditation.

སྤྱོད་པ་མི་མཐུན་རྒྱ་ཆེ་གྲངས་མང་ཡང་། །
CHÖPA MITHÜN GYACHÉ DRANG MANG YANG
Although there are many vast and numerous different lifestyles,

རང་རིག་ཡེ་ཤེས་ཐིག་ལེ་ཉག་གཅིག་ལ། །
RANGRIK YESHE THIGLÉ NYAK CHIK LA
In this single sphere of self-knowing wisdom,

བྱེད་བྱ་དང་ནི་སྤྱོད་བྱེད་གཉིས་སུ་མེད། །
CHEJA DANG NI CHÖJÉ NYISU MÉ
There is no division between doing and doer.

སྤྱོད་པ་མ་བྱེད་སྤྱོད་པའི་མཁན་པོ་ཚོལ། །
CHÖPA MACHÉ CHÖPÉ KHENPO TSÖL
Do not engage in activities, search for the doer.

The Flight of Garuda

སྤྱོད་པའི་མཁན་པོ་བཙལ་བས་མ་རྙེད་ན། །
CHÖPÉ KHENPO TSALWÉ MANYÉ NA
If you search for the doer and do not find him,

དེའི་ཚེ་སྤྱོད་པ་ཟད་སར་འཁྱོལ་བ་ཡིན། །
DÉ TSÉ CHÖPA ZÉSAR KHYÖLWA YIN
At that time, the lifestyle is exhausted.

སྤྱོད་པ་སྤྱད་རྒྱུ་ཅི་ཡང་མེད་པ་ལ། །
CHÖPA CHEGYU CHIYANG MÉPA LA
In the lifestyle where there is nothing whatsoever to practice,

བག་ཆགས་འཁྲུལ་པའི་དབང་དུ་མ་སོང་བར། །
BAKCHAK THRULPÉ WANG DU MASONG WAR
Without falling under the power of habitual delusions,

ད་ལྟའི་ཤེས་པ་མ་བཅོས་རང་གསལ་ལ། །
DA TI SHÉPA MACHÖ RANGSAL LA
This present, unmodified, self-clear awareness,

བཅོས་བསླད་བླང་དོར་གང་ཡང་མི་བྱེད་པ། །
CHÖ LÉ LANGDOR GANG YANG MIJÉ PA
Free from any modification, contamination, accepting, or rejecting,

དེ་ག་རྣམ་པར་དག་པའི་སྤྱོད་པ་ཡིན། །
DÉ GA NAMPAR DAKPÉ CHÖPA YIN
That itself is the perfectly pure lifestyle.

འབྲས་བུ་མི་མཐུན་རྒྱ་ཆེ་གྲངས་མང་ཡང་། །
DREBU MITHÜN GYACHÉ DRANG MANG YANG
Although there are many vast and numerous different results,

Song 19 - Present Awareness

རང་རིག་སྐུ་གསུམ་རྩོལ་མེད་ལྷུན་གྲུབ་ལ། །
RANGRIK KU SUM TSÖLMÉ LHÜNDRUB LA
In the self-knowing three kayas, spontaneously accomplished without effort.

བསྒྲུབ་བྱ་དང་ནི་སྒྲུབ་བྱེད་གཉིས་སུ་མེད། །
DRUBJA DANG NI DRUBJÉ NYISU MÉ
There is no division between result to be attained and attainer.

འབྲས་བུ་མ་སྒྲུབས་སྒྲུབ་པའི་མཁན་པོ་ཚོལ། །
DREBU MADRUB DRUBPÉ KHENPO TSÖL
Do not attain the result, search for the attainer.

འབྲས་བུ་སྒྲུབ་མཁན་བཙལ་བས་མ་རྙེད་ན། །
DREBU DRUBKHEN TSALWÉ MANYÉ NA
If you search for the attainer of the result and do not find her,

དེའི་ཚེ་འབྲས་བུ་ཟད་སར་འཁྱོལ་བ་ཡིན། །
DÉ TSÉ DREBU ZÉSAR KHYÖLWA YIN
At that time, the result reaches its end.

འབྲས་བུ་བསྒྲུབ་རྒྱུ་ཅི་ཡང་མེད་པ་ལ། །
DREBU DRUBGYU CHIYANG MÉPA LA
In the result where there is nothing whatsoever to attain,

བླང་དོར་རེ་དོགས་དབང་དུ་མ་སོང་བར། །
LANGDOR REDOK WANG DU MASONG WAR
Without falling under the power of accepting, rejecting, hope, or fear,

The Flight of Garuda

དལྟའི་ཤེས་རིག་རང་གསལ་ལྷུན་གྲུབ་ཉིད། །
DA TI SHE RIK RANGSAL LHÜNDRUB NYI
This directly present, knowing-awareness, self-clear and spontaneously accomplished,

མངོན་གྱུར་སྐུ་གསུམ་རང་གསལ་སྟོང་པ་ཉིད། །
NGÖNGYUR KU SUM RANGSAL TONGPA NYI
Is the manifest three kayas, self-clear emptiness itself.

ཡེ་སངས་རྒྱས་པའི་འབྲས་བུ་དེ་ཉིད་དོ། །
YE SANG GYÉ PÉ DREBU DÉ NYI DO
That itself is the result of original Buddhahood.

SONG 20

Mastery of Nonduality

༈ ཨེ་མ་ཧོ། ད་ཡང་རིགས་ཀྱི་བུ་རྣམས་ལེགས་པར་ཉོན། །
EMAHO DA YANG RIK KYI BU NAM LEKPAR NYÖN
Emaho! Now again, you of noble lineage, listen well.

དེ་ལྟར་དང་པོ་ཡེངས་མེད་བསྐྱངས་པ་ན། །
DETAR DANGPO YENGMÉ KYANGPA NA
When you have maintained the view in that way without distraction,

བར་དུ་ཡན་པར་བཏང་ཡང་དོན་ཐོག་ནས། །
BARDU YENPAR TANG YANG DÖN THOK NÉ
Then later, let it go freely. In reality,

ཐ་མལ་བཏང་ཡང་འགྲོ་འོང་མེད་པ་འོ། །
THARMAL TANG YANG DRO ONG MÉPA O
Even if you let go in an ordinary way, there is no coming or going.

The Flight of Garuda

སྣང་དང་སྟོང་པ་གཉིས་ཀ་དབྱེར་མེད་ན། །
NANG DANG TONGPA NYI KA YERMÉ NA
When appearance and emptiness are without difference,

དེའི་ཚེ་ལྟ་བ་ཀློང་དུ་གྱུར་པ་ཡིན། །
DÉ TSÉ TAWA LONG DU GYURPA YIN
That is mastery of the view.

རྨི་ལམ་ཉིན་པར་གཉིས་ཀ་ཁྱད་མེད་ན། །
MILAM NYINPAR NYI KA KHYEMÉ NA
When dreams and daytime are without difference,

དེའི་ཚེ་སྒོམ་པ་ཀློང་དུ་གྱུར་པ་ཡིན། །
DÉ TSÉ GOMPA LONG DU GYURPA YIN
That is mastery of the meditation.

བདེ་དང་སྡུག་བསྔལ་གཉིས་ཀ་ཁྱད་མེད་ན། །
DÉ DANG DUKNGAL NYI KA KHYEMÉ NA
When happiness and suffering are without difference,

དེའི་ཚེ་སྤྱོད་པ་ཀློང་དུ་གྱུར་པ་ཡིན། །
DÉ TSÉ CHÖPA LONG DU GYURPA YIN
That is mastery of the lifestyle.

འདི་དང་ཕྱི་མ་གཉིས་ཀ་ཁྱད་མེད་ན། །
DI DANG CHIMA NYI KA KHYEMÉ NA
When this life and the next are without difference,

དེའི་ཚེ་གནས་ལུགས་ཀློང་དུ་གྱུར་པ་ཡིན། །
DÉ TSÉ NELUK LONG DU GYURPA YIN
That is mastery of the natural state.

Song 20 - Mastery of Nonduality

སེམས་དང་ནམ་མཁའ་གཉིས་ཀ་ཁྱད་མེད་ན། །
SEM DANG NAMKHA NYI KA KHYEMÉ NA
When mind and sky are without difference,

དེའི་ཚེ་ཆོས་སྐུ་ཀློང་དུ་གྱུར་པ་ཡིན། །
DÉ TSÉ CHÖKU LONG DU GYURPA YIN
That is mastery of the Dharmakaya.

རང་སེམས་སངས་རྒྱས་གཉིས་ཀ་ཁྱད་མེད་ན། །
RANGSEM SANG GYÉ NYI KA KHYEMÉ NA
When your own mind and Buddha are without difference,

དེའི་ཚེ་འབྲས་བུ་ཀློང་དུ་གྱུར་པ་ཡིན།། །།
DÉ TSÉ DREBU LONG DU GYURPA YIN
That is mastery of the result.

SONG 21

Overcoming Obstacles

ཧཱུྃ ཨེ་མ་ཧོ། ད་དུང་རིགས་ཀྱི་བུ་རྣམས་བདག་ལ་གསོན། །
EMAHO DA DUNG RIK KYI BU NAM DAK LA SÖN
Emaho! Now, you of noble lineage, listen to me.

གདོས་བཅས་ལུས་འདི་ཆུ་ཟླ་ལྟར་དུ་ལྟོས། །
DÖCHÉ LÜ DI CHUZLA TARDU TÖ
See this physical body as being like a reflection of the moon in water.

ངག་གི་སྨྲ་བརྗོད་བྲག་ཆ་བཞིན་དུ་ཉོས། །
NGAK GI MAJÖ BRAKCHA ZHINDU DO
Hear all sounds and speech like an echo.

སེམས་ཀྱི་རྟོག་ཚོགས་རང་སར་སངས་སུ་ཆུག །
SEM KYI TOK TSOK RANGSAR SANG SU CHUK
Let the collection of thoughts in the mind disappear in their own place.

སྣང་གྲགས་ཆོས་རྣམས་ཐམས་ཅད་སྒྱུ་མ་དང་། །
NANGDRAK CHÖ NAM TAMCHÉ GYUMA DANG
All appearances, sounds, and dharmas are like illusions,

སྒྱུག་རྒྱུ་མི་ལམ་གཟུགས་བརྙན་ཆུ་ཟླ་དང་། །
MIKGYU MILAM ZUKNYEN CHUZLA DANG
Like mirages, dreams, reflections of the moon in water,

དྲི་ཟའི་གྲོང་ཁྱེར་མིག་ཡོར་སྤྲུལ་པ་དང་། །
DRIZÉ DRONGKHYER MIKYOR TRULPA DANG
Like cities of Gandharvas, hallucinations, and magical creations,

ཆུ་བུར་བྲག་ཆ་བཞིན་དུ་འཛིན་མེད་སྤྱོད། །
CHUBUR BRAKCHA ZHINDU DZINMÉ CHÖ
Like bubbles and echoes — So, conduct yourself without grasping!

སྤྱོད་ལམ་ཐམས་ཅད་དེ་ཡི་ངང་ནས་གྱིས། །
CHÖLAM TAMCHÉ DÉ YI NGANG NÉ GYI
Engage in all activities within that state.

ཐུན་མཚམས་མ་གཏོགས་ཉིན་མཚན་འཁོར་ཡུག་སྤྲོད། །
THÜNTSAM MACHÖ NYIN TSHEN KHORYUK TRÖ
Don't interrupt sessions, sustain practice continuously day and night.

དྲན་བསམ་བཅོས་བསླད་མ་བྱེད་རང་བབ་ངང་། །
DRENSAM CHÖ LÉ MAJÉ RANGBAB NGANG
Do not fabricate or contaminate thoughts and memories, leave them in their natural state.

རང་མདངས་རང་གྲོལ་འཛིན་མེད་གསལ་སྟོང་དུ། །
RANGDANG RANGDROL DZINMÉ SALTONG DU
In self-radiant, self-liberated, non-grasping clarity and emptiness,

Song 21 - Overcoming Obstacles

བདེན་མེད་སྒོམ་མེད་རྩོལ་མེད་རྗེས་མེད་ཤོག །

DENMÉ GOMMÉ TSÖLMÉ JÉMÉ SHOK

Rest in what is without real existence, without meditation, without effort, without seeking.

སྔར་འདས་རྣམ་པར་རྟོག་པ་ཐམས་ཅད་ཀྱང་། །

NGARDÉ NAMPAR TOKPA TAMCHÉ KYANG

Equally, all past conceptual thoughts —

བྱ་ལམ་ནམ་མཁར་རྗེས་མེད་ལྟར་དུ་ཤོག །

JALAM NAMKHAR JÉMÉ TARDU SHOK

Release them like the path of a bird in the sky, without a trace.

ད་ལྟའི་ཤེས་པ་རྡུལ་བྲལ་བར་སྣང་ལྟར། །

DA TI SHÉPA DÜL DRAL BAR NANG TAR

Just as present awareness appears without any solid particles,

མ་འོངས་རྟོག་པ་རང་འཐག་ཆུ་བཅད་ལྟར། །

MA ONG TOKPA RANGTHAK CHUCHÉ TAR

Future thoughts are like a flow of water which has been suddenly cut off.

ཁྲིག་གེར་གློད་ལ་བཟོ་བཅོས་མི་བྱེད་པར། །

THRIK GER LÖ LA ZOCHÖ MIJÉ PAR

Release and relax without fabricating or modifying.

རང་བབ་རྒྱ་ཡན་ངང་དུ་ལྷུག་པར་ཤོག །

RANGBAB GYAYEN NGANG DU LHUKPAR SHOK

Rest loosely in their natural, vast, and open state.

ཕྲ་རགས་རྟོག་པ་དུག་གསུམ་དུག་ལྔ་སོགས། །
THRARAK TOKPA DUK SUM DUK NGA SOK
Subtle and coarse thoughts, the three poisons, the five toxins, and so on,

ཁང་སྟོང་རྐུན་མ་སླེབས་པ་ལྟར་དུ་ཤོག །
KHANGTONG KÜNMA LEBPA TARDU SHOK
Let them go, like a thief arriving in an empty house.

ཚོགས་དྲུག་ཡུལ་སྣང་ཐམས་ཅད་རྗེས་མེད་དུ། །
TSOK DRUK YÜL NANG TAMCHÉ JÉMÉ DU
All appearances of the objects of the six senses, let them rest without a trace,

སྒྱུ་མའི་གྲོང་ཁྱེར་ཞིག་པ་ལྟར་དུ་ཤོག །
GYÜ MÉ DRONGKHYER ZHIKPA TARDU SHOK
Like the destruction of an illusory city.

མདོར་ན་སྐྱེ་འགག་གནས་གསུམ་གཞི་ལམ་འབྲས། །
DOR NA KYEGAK NÉ SUM ZHILAM DRÉ
In summary, the aspects of arising, abiding, and ceasing; ground, path, and fruition;

ལྟ་སྒོམ་སྤྱོད་འབྲས་དུས་གནས་བརྗོད་ཚིག་དང་། །
TAGOM CHÖDÉ DÜ NÉ JÖTSIK DANG
View, meditation, lifestyle, result; time, location, spoken words,

གཞག་བྱ་འཇོག་བྱེད་དགྲོལ་བྱ་འགྲོལ་བྱེད་སོགས། །
SHAKJA JOKJÉ DROLJA DROLJÉ SOK
Things to be placed, the one who places; things to be liberated, the liberator, and so forth,

Song 21 - Overcoming Obstacles

རང་གསལ་རིས་མེད་འཛིན་རྩོལ་སྤང་བླང་མེད། །
RANGSAL RIMÉ DZIN TSÖL PANGLANG MÉ
In self-clear, unbiased awareness, there is no grasping, effort, abandoning, or adopting.

རྒྱ་མཚོ་ཆེན་པོར་ཆུ་ཕྲན་ཐིམ་པ་ལྟར། །
GYAMTSHO CHENPOR CHUPHREN THIMPA TAR
Just as small streams merges into the great ocean,

ཆོས་ཀུན་སེམས་ཀྱི་དབྱིངས་སུ་ཀ་དག་པར། །
CHÖ KÜN SEM KYI YING SU KADAKPAR
All phenomena are primordially pure in the expanse of mind.

བློ་གདེང་བཅའ་ཞིང་འཛིན་མེད་ལ་བཞག་གོ །
LODENG CHA ZHING DZINMÉ LA DLA O
Establish confidence and return to non-grasping.

དེ་ལྟར་སྒོམ་ཚེ་རྣམ་རྟོག་མང་འཕྲོས་ཀྱང་། །
DETAR GOM TSÉ NAMTOK MANG THRÖ KYANG
When you meditate in that way, even if many conceptual thoughts arise,

སྒོམ་ནི་མ་འོངས་སྙམ་ནས་སྡུག་མི་དགོས། །
GOM NI MA ONG NYAM NÉ DUK MI GÖ
Do not be upset thinking, "Meditation is not working."

སེམས་ནི་འཕྲོ་ཡང་སྟོང་ལ་གནས་ཀྱང་སྟོང་། །
SEM NI THRO YANG TONG LA NÉ KYANG TONG
Mind, even when it moves, it is empty; when it is still, it is empty.

The Flight of Garuda

གང་ལྟར་ཤར་ཡང་རིག་པའི་ངང་ཡིན་པས། །
GANGTAR SHAR YANG RIGPÉ NGANG YIN PÉ
However it arises, since it is the state of rigpa itself,

དགག་སྒྲུབ་བླང་དོར་གང་ཡང་མི་བྱེད་པར། །
GAKDRUB LANGDOR GANG YANG MIJÉ PAR
Without affirming, denying, accepting, or rejecting,

མ་བཅོས་གཉུག་མའི་ངང་དུ་གློད་ལ་ཞོག །
MACHÖ NYUKMÉ NGANG DU LÖ LA SHOK
Release and rest in the unmodified, natural state.

དེ་ཡིས་རྣམ་རྟོག་རང་སར་གྲོལ་བར་ངེས། །
DÉ YI NAMTOK RANGSAR DROLWAR NGÉ
By that, conceptual thoughts will certainly be liberated in their own place.

བློ་དམན་སྐྱེ་བོ་ངང་ལ་མི་གནས་ན། །
LODMEN KYEWO NGANG LA MI NÉ NA
If people of lesser capacity can't abide in this state,

ངོ་སྤྲོད་སྐབས་བཞིན་དཔྱད་འཇོག་སླེལ་མ་གྱིས། །
NGOTRÖ KAB ZHIN PÉ JOK PELMA GYI
As at the time of introduction, alternate between investigating and resting.

ཡང་ན་འདི་བཞིན་རྣམ་རྟོག་འར་ལ་གཏོད། །
YANG NA DI ZHIN NAMTOK AR LA TÖ
Or else, in this way, entrust thoughts to thoughts:

Song 21 - Overcoming Obstacles

དགོས་སམ་མི་དགོས་རྣམ་རྟོག་བསྐྱེད་ནས་ཀྱང་། །
GÖ SAM MI GÖ NAMTOK LÉ NÉ KYANG
Pushing the conceptual mind to it's breaking point,

གཅིག་རྗེས་གཅིག་མཐུད་རྣམ་པ་སྣ་ཚོགས་པ། །
CHIK JÉ CHIK THÜ NAMPA NATSOKPA
Generate a variety of thoughts one after another,

རང་སེམས་སུན་རག་བར་དུ་སྤྲོས་ནས་ཀྱང་། །
RANGSEM SÜNRAK WARDU TRÖ NÉ KYANG
Elaborating them until your own mind is exhausted (or bored).

དེ་ནས་མི་འདོད་ཚེ་ན་གློད་ལ་ཞོག །
DÉ NÉ MIDÖ TSÉ NA LÖ LA SHOK
Then, when you have no energy to continue, release them, and rest freely.

ཡང་ན་སྙིང་དབུས་མཚན་ལྡན་བླ་མ་བསྒོམས། །
YANG NA NYINGWÜ TSHEN DEN LAMA GOM
Or, you can meditate on the authentic guru in the center of your heart.

དེ་ལ་སེམས་ནི་ཡུན་རིང་བཟུང་ནས་ཀྱང་། །
DÉ LA SEM NI YÜN RING ZUNG NÉ KYANG
After concentrating your mind on that for a long time,

དེ་རྗེས་འཛིན་མེད་རིག་པའི་ངང་ལ་ཞོག །
DÉ JÉ DZINMÉ RIGPÉ NGANG LA SHOK
Then, rest in the state of non-grasping awareness.

ཡང་ན་སྙིང་གི་དབུས་སུ་ཐིག་ལེ་སྒོམས། །
YANG NA NYING GI WÜ SU THIGLÉ GOM
Or, you can meditate on a sphere of light (*thiglé*) in the center of your heart:

དེ་ཉིད་མར་ལ་བབས་ནས་དབང་ཆེན་གྱི། །
DÉ NYI MAR LA BAB NÉ WANGCHEN GYI
Visualize that it descends downwards,

ས་གཞིར་ཐུག་རག་བར་དུ་སོང་བར་བསམ། །
SA ZHIR THUKRAK BARDU SONGWAR SAM
And goes all the way down to touch the great ground.

དེ་ཡིས་འཕྲོ་གོད་བྱེད་ཀྱིས་ཆོད་པར་ངེས། །
DÉ YI THRO GÖ BÉ KYI CHÖPAR NGÉ
By that, wild thoughts, and agitation will definitely be ended.

གོད་པ་ཆོད་ཚེ་རིག་པའི་ངང་ལ་ཞོག །
GÖPA CHÖ TSÉ RIGPÉ NGANG LA SHOK
When agitation is gone, rest in the state of awareness.

བྱིང་བ་ཆེ་ན་ལྟ་སྟངས་དར་བསྐྱེད་ལ། །
JINGWA CHÉ NA TATANG NGAR KYÉ LA
If dullness is strong, sharpen your gaze.

རིག་པ་རྗེན་ལ་ཕྱུད་ནས་སལེར་སྐྱོངས། །
RIGPA JEN LA PHÜ NÉ SALER KYONG
Leave awareness naked and maintain it with clarity.

Song 21 - Overcoming Obstacles

ཡང་ན་རང་གི་སེམས་ཉིད་ཐིག་ལེ་རུ། །
YANG NA RANG GI SEMNYI THIGLÉ RU
Or, you can visualize your own mind as a *thiglé*:

དམིགས་ལ་དག་ནས་ཕཊ་སྒྲ་བརྗོད་མ་ཐག །
MIK LA NGAK NÉ PHAT DRA JÖ MATHAK
Focus on it clearly, then suddenly utter the sound PHET!

ཚངས་བུག་ནས་ཐོན་དཔག་ཆེན་མདའ་འཕངས་ལྟར། །
TSANGBUK NÉ THÖN PAKCHEN DA PHANG TAR
Think that it comes out from the crown point like a great arrow shot,

སོང་ནས་མཁའ་ལ་འཁྲུག་གིས་འདྲེས་པར་བསམ། །
SONG NÉ KHA LA THRUK GI DRÉPAR SAM
Mixing completely with the sky.

དེ་ནས་ནམ་མཁའི་མཚན་ཉིད་ཡིད་ལ་གྱིས། །
DÉ NÉ NAMKHÉ TSHENNYI YID LA GYI
Then, bring the qualities of the sky to your mind.

དེ་ཡིས་བྱིང་བ་མི་སངས་མི་སྲིད་དོ། །
DÉ YI JINGWA MI SANG MISID DO
By that, dullness will definitely not remain.

བྱིང་བ་སངས་ཚེ་འཛིན་མེད་ངང་ལ་ཞོག །
JINGWA SANG TSÉ DZINMÉ NGANG LA SHOK
When dullness clears, rest in the state of non-grasping.

འདི་རྣམས་ཞལ་ཤེས་ཡིན་པས་ཤེས་པར་གྱིས། །
DI NAM SHALSHÉ YIN PÉ SHÉPAR GYI
Know that these are oral instructions.

ཐོག་མེད་འདོད་པ་ཐོག་པས་མ་བཅིངས་པར། །
TOKMÉ DÖPA TOKPÉ MACHING PAR
Without being bound by the thought of wanting to be free from thought,

རིག་པ་རྒྱ་བསྐྱེད་དཔངས་བསྟོད་ཆལ་ཡས་སུ། །
RIGPA GYAKYÉ PANGTÖ CHALYÉ SU
Expand awareness beyond measure, open more and more,

ཐོངས་ལ་གུ་ཡངས་ཡན་པ་གློད་བདེ་གྱིས། །
THONG LA GUYANG YENPA LODÉ GYI
Then, release it and be comfortable with vast openness and freedom.

དང་པོ་རྣམ་རྟོག་གཙོང་རོང་ཆུ་དང་འདྲ། །
DANGPO NAMTOK CHONGRONG CHU DANG DRA
In the beginning, conceptual thoughts are like water rushing in a narrow gorge.

བར་དུ་ཆུ་བོ་གངྒཱ་དལ་འབབ་འདྲ། །
BARDU CHUWO GANGGA DALBAB DRA
In the middle, they are like the steady flow of the Ganges River.

ཐ་མ་ཆུ་རྣམས་རྒྱ་མཚོར་རོ་གཅིག་ལྟར། །
THAMA CHU NAM GYAMTSHOR ROCHIK TAR
In the end, thoughts are like all waters becoming one taste in the ocean.

འོད་གསལ་མ་བུ་མཇལ་བའི་ངང་ལ་གནས། །
ÖSAL MAWU JELWÉ NGANG LA NÉ
Rest in the state of the bonding of clear light mother and child.

Song 21 - Overcoming Obstacles

ཁྱད་པར་ནད་གདོན་ཆོ་འཕྲུལ་ཅི་བྱུང་ཡང༌། །
KHYEPAR NEDÖN CHÖTHRUL CHI JUNG YANG
Especially whatever illness, harmful influence, or magical display occurs,

བཅས་བཅོས་རིམ་གྲོ་གང་ཡང་མི་བྱེད་པར། །
CHÉ CHÖ RIMDRO GANG YANG MIJÉ PAR
Without doing any forced remedies or rituals,

འདི་ལྟར་རོ་སྙོམས་ཐོག་བཟི་སྤྱོད་པ་གྱིས། །
DITAR RONYOM THOK DZI CHÖPA GYI
Practice in this way, treating everything with equanimity.

ནགས་དང་དུར་ཁྲོད་མཚོ་གླིང་སྐྱེད་མོའི་ཚལ། །
NAK DANG DURTHRÖ TSHO LING KYEMÖ TSHAL
In forests, charnel grounds, islands, beautiful groves,

བྲག་ཕུག་ཁང་སྟོང་ཤིང་གཅིག་དྲུང་ལ་སོགས། །
BRAKPHUK KHANGTONG SHINGCHIK DRUNG LA SOK
Rock caves, empty houses, at the foot of a solitary tree, and so forth.

འཇིགས་ཤིང་ཉམ་ངའི་གནས་སུ་སོང་ནས་ཀྱང༌། །
JIK ZHING NYANGÉ NÉ SU SONG NÉ KYANG
After going to places that you feel danger, panic, or discomfort,

རང་ལུས་སྣོད་བཅུད་སྣང་སྲིད་བདུད་རྩིར་བསྒྱུར། །
RANGLÜ NÖCHÜ NANGSRI DÜTSIR GYUR
Transform your own body, the contents of the world, and all existence into nectar.

ཕྱོགས་བཅུའི་རྒྱལ་བ་སྲས་བཅས་ཐམས་ཅད་མཆོད། །
CHOK CHÜ GYALWA SÉ CHÉ TAMCHÉ CHÖ
Offer it to all the Buddhas of the ten directions together with their Bodhisattvas.

དེ་རྣམས་མཉེས་ནས་བརྩེ་བའི་རྣམ་འགྱུར་གྱིས། །
DÉ NAM NYÉ NÉ TSEWÉ NAMGYUR GYI
When they are pleased, with an expression of love,

འོད་དུ་ཞུ་ནས་འཁོར་འདས་ཐམས་ཅད་ཀུན། །
Ö DU ZHU NÉ KHORDÉ TAMCHÉ KÜN
Visualize that all of samsara and nirvana dissolve into light,

འོད་གསལ་བདུད་རྩིས་ཡོངས་སུ་གང་བར་དམིགས། །
ÖSAL DÜTSI YONG SU GANGWAR MIK
See them as being completely filled with the nectar of clear light.

ཡོན་ཏན་མགྲོན་གྱུར་དམ་ཅན་ཆོས་སྐྱོང་དང་། །
YÖNTEN DRÖN GYUR DAMCHEN CHÖKYONG DANG
The Oath-bound Dharma protectors, guests of quality,

སྙིང་རྗེའི་ཞིང་མཆོག་རིགས་དྲུག་སེམས་ཅན་དང་། །
NYINGJÉ ZHINGCHOK RIK DRUK SEMCHEN DANG
The supreme field of compassion, the sentient beings of the six realms,

ལན་ཆགས་གདོན་བགེགས་འབྱུང་པོ་ཐམས་ཅད་དང་། །
LANCHAK DÖNGEK JUNGPO TAMCHÉ DANG
All those with karmic debts, harmful spirits, obstacle-makers, and elementals,

Song 21 - Overcoming Obstacles

ནམ་མཁའི་མཐར་དང་མཉམ་པའི་འགྲོ་བ་ཀུན། །
NAMKHÉ THA DANG NYAMPÉ DROWA KÜN
All beings equal to the extent of space,

མྱོང་གྲོལ་བདུད་རྩིས་ཚིམས་པར་བྱས་ནས་ཀྱང་། །
NYONGDROL DÜTSI TSHIMPAR JÉ NÉ KYANG
After satisfying them with the nectar which liberates by taste,

འཁོར་འདས་རོ་གཅིག་སེམས་སུ་ཐག་བཅད་ལ། །
KHORDÉ ROCHIK SEM SU THAKCHÉ LA
Decide that samsara and nirvana are of one taste in the mind.

སེམས་ཉིད་མ་བཅོས་ཆོས་སྐུའི་ངང་ཉིད་ནས། །
SEMNYI MACHÖ CHÖKÜ NGANG NYI NÉ
From the very state of the unfabricated mind, Dharmakaya itself,

འགྲོ་དང་འདུག་དང་མཆོངས་དང་རྒྱུག་པ་དང་། །
DRO DANG DUK DANG CHONG DANG GYUKPA DANG
Walk, sit, jump, run,

སྐད་དང་དགོད་དང་ངུ་དང་གླུ་ལེན་དང་། །
DRA DANG GÖ DANG NGU DANG LULEN DANG
Speak, laugh, cry, sing,

བཅགས་དང་དཀྲུག་ལོག་སྨྱོན་པའི་སྤྱོད་པ་བྱ། །
CHAK DANG DRUK LOK NYÖNPÉ CHÖPA JA
Break things, cause chaos, act like a mad person,

མཐར་ནི་ཞི་ཞིང་བདེ་བའི་ངང་ལ་འདུག །
THAR NI ZHI ZHING DEWÉ NGANG LA DUK
Finally, rest freely in a state of peace and happiness.

མཚན་དུས་རང་བབ་བདེ་བར་ཉལ་ནས་ཀྱང་། །
TSHEN DÜ RANGBAB DEWAR NYAL NÉ KYANG
At night, after falling peacefully asleep,

དྲན་བསམ་འཕྲོ་འདུའི་རྣམ་རྟོག་ཀུན་བྲལ་ཏེ། །
DRENSAM THRO DÜ NAMTOK KÜNDRAL TÉ
Completely free from all conceptual thoughts and memories,

སྐྱེ་མེད་དྲན་རྫོགས་གཉུག་མའི་ངང་ལ་ཉལ། །
KYEMÉ DREN DZOK NYUKMÉ NGANG LA NYAL
Sleep in the unborn, fully aware, natural state.

དེ་ལྟར་བྱས་ན་ནད་གདོན་རང་ཞི་ནས། །
DETAR JÉ NA NEDÖN RANG ZHI NÉ
If you do these things, illnesses and harmful influences will naturally subside.

ལྟ་སྒོམ་བོགས་འབྱིན་རྟོགས་པ་ནམ་མཁའ་འདྲ། །
TAGOM BOKJIN TOKPA NAMKHA DRA
View and meditation will improve, realization will be like the sky.

སྒོམ་པ་རང་གསལ་སྤྱོད་པ་བུ་ཆུང་འདྲ། །
GOMPA RANGSAL CHÖPA BU CHUNG DRA
Meditation will be self-clear, the way of living will be playful like a young child.

གཟའ་གཏད་ཀུན་བྲལ་རང་གིས་སྨྱོན་པ་འདྲ། །
ZATÉ KÜNDRAL NGANG GI NYÖNPA DRA
Being free from all fixation, spontaneous like a mad person,

Song 21 - Overcoming Obstacles

བདག་གཞན་གཉིས་མེད་འཕགས་པའི་གང་ཟག་འདྲ། །

DAKSHEN NYIMÉ PHAKPÉ GANGZAK DRA

Like a noble being who sees no separation between self and other,

ཅི་སྨྲ་འཛིན་མེད་བྲག་ཆའི་སྒྲ་དབྱངས་འདྲ། །

CHI DRA DZINMÉ BRAKCHÉ DRA YANG DRA

Whatever you say will be like the sound of an echo, without grasping,

གང་ལའང་ཆགས་མེད་འདབ་ཆགས་མཁའ་ལྡིང་འདྲ། །

GANG LA'ANG CHAKMÉ DABCHAK KHADING DRA

Without attachment to anything, like a garuda soaring in the sky.

ཡ་ང་བག་ཚ་མེད་པ་སེང་གེ་འདྲ། །

YA NGA BAKTSA MÉPA SENGGÉ DRA

Without fear or hesitation, like a lion.

ཐམས་ཅད་ཡེ་གྲོལ་མཁའ་ལ་སྤྲིན་དངས་འདྲ། །

TAMCHÉ YEDROL KHA LA TRIN DANG DRA

All is primordially liberated, like a sky clear of clouds.

དེ་འདྲའི་རྣལ་འབྱོར་བདེ་གཤེགས་རིག་འཛིན་དངོས། །

DI DRA'I NALJOR DESHEK RIGDZIN NGÖ

Such a yogi is a genuine Sugata and Vidyadhara,

དད་བརྒྱའི་སྤྱི་བོས་བཏུད་ནས་ཕྱག་བྱའི་འོས། །

DAD GYÉ CHIWÖ TÜ NÉ CHAKJÉ Ö

Worthy of being honored with a hundredfold faith at the crown of the head.

ཡིད་བཞིན་ནོར་བུ་བས་ཀྱང་ཆེས་ལྷག་གོ། །

YIZHIN NORBU WÉ KYANG CHÉ LHAK GO

They are even more precious than a wish-fulfilling jewel.

SONG 22

The Five Buddhas are Within

ཧཱུྃ༔ ཨེ་མ་ཧོ། ད་ཡང་སྐལ་ལྡན་བྱ་བཏང་བླུ་ལ་ཉོན། །
EMAHO DA YANG KALDEN JATANG LU LA NYÖN
Emaho! Now again, fortunate renunciates, listen to this song.

རྣམ་སྣང་ཕྱི་ན་མེད་དེ་ནང་ན་ཡོད། །
NAM NANG CHI NA MÉ DÉ NANG NA YÖ
Vairochana is not outside, he is inside, within yourself.

སེམས་ཉིད་སྤྲོས་དང་བྲལ་བ་ཆོས་དབྱིངས་ངང་། །
SEMNYI TRÖ DANG DRALWA CHÖYING NGANG
Mind itself, free from elaboration, in the state of the expanse of reality,

གཏི་མུག་རང་སར་དག་པའི་ངོ་བོ་ཉིད། །
TIMUK RANGSAR DAKPÉ NGOWO NYI
The very essence of ignorance, pure in its own place,

བཅོམ་ལྡན་རྣམ་པར་སྣང་མཛད་དངོས་ཡིན་ནོ། །
CHOMDEN NAMPAR NANGDZÉ NGÖ YIN NO
This is truly Buddha Vairochana.

The Flight of Garuda

རྡོར་སེམས་ཕྱི་ན་མེད་དེ་ནང་ན་ཡོད། །
DORSEM CHI NA MÉ DÉ NANG NA YÖ
Vajrasattva is not outside, he is inside, within yourself.

རིག་རྩལ་འཆར་གཞི་མ་འགགས་མེ་ལོང་དང་། །
RIG TZAL CHARZHI MAAKAK MELONG DANG
The unceasing display of the power of awareness is like a mirror.

ཞེ་སྡང་རང་སར་དག་པའི་ངོ་བོ་ཉིད། །
SHEDANG RANGSAR DAKPÉ NGOWO NYI
The very essence of anger itself, pure in its own place,

བཅོམ་ལྡན་རྡོ་རྗེ་སེམས་དཔའ་དངོས་ཡིན་ནོ། །
CHOMDEN DORJÉ SEMPA NGÖ YIN NO
This is truly Buddha Vajrasattva.

རིན་འབྱུང་ཕྱི་ན་མེད་དེ་ནང་ན་ཡོད། །
RINCHUNG CHI NA MÉ DÉ NANG NA YÖ
Ratnasambhava is not outside, he is inside, within yourself.

བླང་དོར་དགག་སྒྲུབ་མེད་པ་མཉམ་ཉིད་ངང་། །
LANGDOR GAKDRUB MÉPA NYAMNYI NGANG
The state of equality, without accepting or rejecting, affirming or denying,

ང་རྒྱལ་རང་སར་དག་པའི་ངོ་བོ་ཉིད། །
NGAGYAL RANGSAR DAKPÉ NGOWO NYI
The very essence of pride itself, pure in its own place,

Song 22 - The Five Buddhas are Within

བཅོམ་ལྡན་རིན་ཆེན་འབྱུང་ལྡན་དངོས་ཡིན་ནོ། །
CHOMDEN RINCHEN JUNGDEN NGÖ YIN NO
This is truly Buddha Ratnasambhava.

འོད་དཔག་ཕྱི་ན་མེད་དེ་ནང་ན་ཡོད། །
ÖPAK CHI NA MÉ DÉ NANG NA YÖ
Amitabha is not outside, he is inside, within yourself.

བདེ་སྟོང་དབྱིངས་སུ་ནུབ་པ་སོར་རྟོག་ངང་། །
DETONG YING SU NUBPA SORTOK NGANG
The state of discriminating awareness, immersed in the expanse of bliss and emptiness.

འདོད་ཆགས་རང་སར་དག་པའི་ངོ་བོ་ཉིད། །
DÖCHAK RANGSAR DAKPÉ NGOWO NYI
The very essence of desire itself, pure in its own place,

བཅོམ་ལྡན་འོད་དཔག་མེད་པ་དངོས་ཡིན་ནོ། །
CHOMDEN ÖPAK MÉPA NGÖ YIN NO
This is truly Buddha Amitabha.

དོན་གྲུབ་ཕྱི་ན་མེད་དེ་ནང་ན་ཡོད། །
DÖNDRUB CHI NA MÉ DÉ NANG NA YÖ
Amoghasiddhi is not outside, he is inside, within yourself.

རིག་པ་ཐལ་བྱུང་རང་གྲོལ་བྱ་གྲུབ་ངང་། །
RIGPA THALJUNG RANGDROL JA DRUB NGANG
The state of spontaneously arising awareness, self-liberated, already perfectly accomplished,

The Flight of Garuda

ཕྲག་དོག་རང་སར་དག་པའི་ངོ་བོ་ཉིད། །
THRAKDOK RANGSAR DAKPÉ NGOWO NYI
The very essence of jealousy itself, pure in its own place,

བཅོམ་ལྡན་དོན་ཡོད་གྲུབ་པ་དངོས་ཡིན་ནོ།། །།
CHOMDEN DÖNYÖ DRUBPA NGÖ YIN NO
This is truly Buddha Amoghasiddhi.

SONG 23

Life is the Teaching

ཧཱུྃ ཨེ་མ་ཧོ། ད་ཡང་སྐལ་ལྡན་སེམས་ཀྱི་བུ་གཅིག་པོ། །
EMAHO DA YANG KALDEN SEM KYI BU CHIKPO
Emaho! Now again, fortunate, only child of my heart,

དགའ་ཞིང་སྤྲོ་བས་རྡོ་རྗེའི་གླུ་ལ་ཉོན། །
GA ZHING TROWÉ DORJÉ LU LA NYÖN
Listen with joy and enthusiasm to this vajra song.

དེ་ལྟར་རྟོགས་ན་སྣང་སྲིད་ཐམས་ཅད་ཀུན། །
DETAR TOK NA NANGSRI TAMCHÉ KÜN
If you understand just this, all of appearance and existence,

གདམས་ངག་དཔེ་ཆ་དོན་གྱི་དཀྱིལ་འཁོར་ཡིན། །
DAMNGAK PECHA DÖN GYI KYILKHOR YIN
Are the instructions, books, and the mandala of meaning.

སྣང་བ་དཀར་དམར་སྣ་ཚོགས་ཤོག་གུ་ལ། །
NANGWA KARMAR NATSOK SHOGGU LA
On the paper of various white, red, and other appearances,

The Flight of Garuda

རང་བྱུང་ཡེ་ཤེས་རིག་པའི་སྨྱུ་གུ་ཡིས། །
RANGJUNG YESHE RIGPÉ NYUGU YI
With the pen of self-arising wisdom awareness,

གཞི་མེད་ཡེ་གྲོལ་འཛིན་མེད་ཡི་གེ་བྲིས། །
ZHIMÉ YEDROL DZINMÉ YIGÉ DRI
Write the letters of baseless, primordially liberated, non-grasping.

སྣང་སྟོང་གཉིས་མེད་ངང་དུ་དཔེ་བལྟས་བྱས། །
NANGTONG NYIMÉ NGANG DU PÉ TÉ JA
Look at the book in the state of inseparable appearance and emptiness.

སྟོང་གསུམ་ཐམས་ཅད་ལྷུན་གྲུབ་དཀྱིལ་འཁོར་ལ། །
TONGSUM TAMCHÉ LHÜNDRUB KYILKHOR LA
On the spontaneously accomplished mandala of all three thousand worlds,

ཆར་ཆུ་རང་བབ་ཆུ་ཡིས་ཆག་ཆག་གདབ། །
CHARCHU RANGBAB CHU YI CHAKCHAK DAB
Rain naturally sprinkles down.

ལམ་སྲང་རང་བཞིན་ཐིག་ཆེན་གདབ་པ་དང་། །
LAM SANG RANGSHIN THIK CHEN DABPA DANG
The nature of roads and paths are like the marking of essential points.

རྐང་པའི་རྗེས་ནི་ཁ་དོག་རྡུལ་ཚོན་རིས། །
KANGPÉ JÉ NI KHADOK DÜL TSON RI
Footprints are like drawings made with colored sand.

Song 23 - Life is the Teaching

རང་ལུས་སྣང་སྟོང་ཡི་དམ་ལྷ་ཡི་སྐུ། །
RANGLÜ NANGTONG YIDAM LHA YI KU
Your own body (appearance-emptiness), is the form of the yidam deity.

སྨྲ་བརྗོད་གྲགས་སྟོང་རྡོ་རྗེའི་བཟླས་པ་དང་། །
MAJÖ DRAK TONG DORJÉ DZEPA DANG
Speech, the sound of emptiness, is the vajra recitation.

དྲན་བསམ་འཛིན་མེད་རང་གྲོལ་ལྷ་ཡི་ཐུགས། །
DRENSAM DZINMÉ RANGDROL LHA YI THUK
Thoughts and memories, non-grasping, self-liberated, are the mind of the deity.

ཡན་ལག་འགུལ་བསྐྱོད་ཐམས་ཅད་ཕྱག་རྒྱ་འོ། །
YENLAK GÜLKYÖ TAMCHÉ CHAKGYA O
All movements of the limbs are mudras.

བཟའ་དང་བཏུང་བ་ཆོས་ཉིད་མཆོད་པ་དང་། །
ZA DANG TUNGWA CHÖNYI CHÖPA DANG
Eating and drinking are true natural offerings.

གཟུགས་སུ་སྣང་བ་ཐམས་ཅད་ལྷ་ཡི་སྐུ། །
ZUK SU NANGWA TAMCHÉ LHA YI KU
All that appears as form is the deity's body.

སྒྲ་ཆེན་བརྗོད་པ་ཐམས་ཅད་རོལ་མོ་ཉིད། །
DRA CHEN JÖPA TAMCHÉ ROLMO NYI
All sounds expressed are music itself.

བསྲུང་མེད་ཉམས་མེད་རང་བབ་དམ་ཚིག་གོ། །
SUNGMÉ NYAMMÉ RANGBAB DAMTSIK GO
The samaya is the natural state which needs no guarding or keeping.

དེ་འདྲའི་རྣལ་འབྱོར་པ་ཡིས་ཅི་བྱས་ཀྱང་། །
DI DRA'I NALJORPA YI CHI JÉ KYANG
Whatever such a yogi does,

འོད་གསལ་ཆོས་ཉིད་ངང་ལ་གདམས་ངག་དང་། །
ÖSAL CHÖNYI NGANG LA DAM NGAK DANG
In the natural state of clear light, the oral instructions,

བསྐྱེད་རིམ་དམ་ཚིག་དང་བཅས་རྫོགས་པས་ན། །
KYÉRIM DAMTSIK DANG CHÉ DZOK PÉ NA
Including the generation stage and samayas are complete within it —

འབད་རྩོལ་རྒྱུ་འབྲས་ཆོས་ལ་བརྟེན་མི་དགོས། །
BÉTSÖL GYUDRÉ CHÖ LA TEN MI GÖ
He does not need to rely on effort, the karmic dharma, or other practices.

འབད་མེད་དངོས་གྲུབ་ཡ་མཚན་རྨད་པོ་ཆེ། །
BÉ MÉ NGÖDRUB YATSHEN MAPOCHE
Effortless accomplishment, miraculous and wonderful,

མྱུར་དུ་འཐོབ་པ་རྫོགས་པ་ཆེན་པོ་ཡི། །
NYURDU THOBPA DZOGPA CHENPO YI
To quickly obtain this is the characteristic of Dzogchen.

Song 23 - Life is the Teaching

ཁྱད་ཆོས་ཡིན་ནོ་སྐལ་ལྡན་སྙིང་གི་བུ། །
KHYECHÖ YIN NO KALDEN NYING GI BU
This is its special quality, fortunate heart child.

དེ་ལྟར་ངེས་པར་ཉམས་སུ་བླང་གྱུར་ན། །
DETAR NGEPAR NYAM SU LANG GYUR NA
If you definitely practice in that way,

སྤྲིན་རྣམས་ནམ་མཁའི་དངལ་ལ་ཡལ་བ་བཞིན། །
TRIN NAM NAMKHÉ NGANG LA YALWA ZHIN
Just as clouds dissolve in the state of the sky,

འཁོར་འདས་རྟོགས་ཚོགས་གདོད་མའི་གཞི་ལ་དག །
KHORDÉ TOKTSHOK DÖMÉ ZHI LA DAK
The collections of realizations of samsara and nirvana are purified in the primordial ground.

ཉི་མའི་དཀྱིལ་འཁོར་སྒྲིབ་མེད་གསལ་བ་བཞིན། །
NYI MÉ KYILKHOR DRIBMÉ SALWA ZHIN
Just as the sun's mandala is clear without obscuration.

རང་རིག་འོད་གསལ་ཆོས་སྐུ་མངོན་གྱུར་ནས། །
RANGRIK ÖSAL CHÖKU NGÖNGYUR NÉ
Self-knowing clear light, the Dharmakaya, will become manifest.

བསད་པ་གསོ་ནུས་གསང་བ་གོ་ནུས་ཤིང་། །
SÉPA SONO NÜ SANGWA GO NÜ ZHING
You will gain the power of revival and become clairvoyant,

རྫུ་འཕྲུལ་སྣ་ཚོགས་བསྟན་ནས་འགྲོ་བ་འདུལ། །
DZUPHRUL NATSOK TEN NÉ DROWA DUL
Show various miraculous powers and tame beings.

ས་ལམ་ཡོན་ཏན་མ་ལུས་རབ་རྫོགས་ནས། །
SA LAM YÖNTEN MALÜ RABDZOK NÉ
Having perfectly completed all the qualities of the stages and paths,

གང་ཟག་དབང་པོ་རབ་རྣམས་ཚེ་འདིར་གྲོལ། །
GANGZAK WANGPO RAB NAM TSÉ DIR DROL
Those individuals with the highest faculties will be liberated in this lifetime.

འབྲིང་ནི་འཆི་ཁ་ཐ་མ་བར་དོ་རུ། །
DRING NI CHIKHA THAMA BARDO RU
Those of intermediate capacity will be liberated at the final moment of death, or lesser ones in the bardo.

ཀ་དག་གཞི་ལ་གྲོལ་ནས་ནང་དབྱིངས་སུ། །
KADAK ZHI LA DROL NÉ NANG YING SU
Having been liberated in the primordially pure ground, into the inner expanse,

སྐུ་གསུམ་ཡེ་ཤེས་འབྲལ་མེད་རྟག་བཞུགས་ནས། །
KU SUM YESHE DRALMÉ TAK SHYUK NÉ
The three kayas and wisdoms will remain inseparable.

གང་ལ་གང་འདུལ་སྤྲུལ་པ་བསྐྱེད་ནས་ཀྱང་། །
GANG LA GANG DUL TRULPA KYÉ NÉ KYANG
After emanating whatever emanations are needed to tame beings,

འགྲོ་དོན་རྒྱུན་མི་འཆད་པར་མཛད་པ་འོ། །
DÖDÖN GYÜN MICHÉ PAR DZÉPA O
They will continuously perform the benefit of beings.

Song 23 - Life is the Teaching

ཚིག་དོན་འདི་རྣམས་ཡིད་ལ་ཟུངས་ཤིག་དང་། །
TSIK DÖN DI NAM YID LA ZUNG SHIG DANG
Remember these profound words and meanings.

སྐྱིད་པའི་ཉི་མ་ནང་ནས་འཆར་བར་དེས། །
KYIPÉ NYIMA NANG NÉ CHARWAR NGÉ
The sun of happiness will definitely rise from within.

དེ་འདྲའི་དགོངས་པ་གླུ་རུ་ལེན་མཁན་དེ། །
DI DRA'I GONGPA LU RU LENKHEN DÉ
The one who sings such realization as a song,

བྱ་བཏང་ཚོགས་དྲུག་རང་གྲོལ་ཡིན་པར་སྣང་། །
JATANG TSOK DRUK RANGDROL YINPAR NANG
Appears to be the renunciate Tsokdruk Rangdrol,

དགེ་འདིས་སྐལ་ལྡན་གདུལ་བྱ་མང་པོ་ཡི། །
GÉ DI KALDEN DÜLJA MANGPO YI
For many fortunate disciples, may this merit cause,

མ་རིག་ཉོན་མོངས་རྟོག་པའི་དྲི་མ་ཀུན། །
MARIG NYÖNMONG TOKPÉ DRIMA KÜN
All the stains of ignorance, afflictions, and conceptual thoughts,

ཀ་དག་གདོད་མའི་དབྱིངས་སུ་མྱུར་དག་ནས། །
KADAK DÖMÉ YING SU NYUR DAK NÉ
To be quickly purified in the expanse of primordial purity.

འབྲས་བུ་ཚེ་འདི་ཉིད་ལ་འཐོབ་པར་ཤོག
DRÉBU TSÉ DI NYI LA THOBPAR SHOK
And may they attain the result in this very lifetime.

|ཅེས་འོད་གསལ་རྫོགས་པ་ཆེན་པོའི་ཁྲེགས་ཆོད་ལྟ་བའི་གླུ་དབྱངས་ས་ལམ་མྱུར་དུ་བགྲོད་
པའི་ཁྲུལ་ལྡན་མཁའ་ལྡིང་གཤོག་རླབས་ཞེས་བྱ་བ་འདི་ནི།

Thus, this song of the Trekchö view of the Great Perfection of Clear Light, called "The Flight of Garuda for Swiftly Traversing the Stages and Paths,"

ཨོ་རྒྱན་རིན་པོ་ཆེས་མཛད་པའི་རིག་པ་གཅེར་མཐོང་གི་དོ་སྲོང༌། ཀུན་མཁྱེན་མཛོད་བདུན་
དང་ཤིང་རྟ་གསུམ། རྫོགས་ཆེན་རྒྱབ་ཆོས་ནས་མཁའ་སྐོར་གསུམ། ཟབ་དོན་རྒྱ་མཚོའི་
སྤྲིན་ཕུང༌། རྫོགས་ཆེན་མཁའ་འགྲོའི་སྙིང་ཐིག །སངས་རྒྱས་ལག་བཅངས་སོགས་གཏེར་ཁ་
དུ་མའི་རྫོགས་ཆེན་མན་ངག་ལ་གཞི་བྱས།

བླ་མའི་མན་ངག་དང་རང་གི་ཉམས་མྱོང་གིས་བྲུར་བརྒྱན་ཏེ་

Is based on the 'Direct Introduction to Naked Awareness' by Orgyen Rinpoche [13], the 'Seven Treasuries' and 'Three Chariots' of Omniscient Longchenpa [14], the 'Three Cycles of Space' of the Dzogchen Gyabcho, the 'Cloud Bank of the Ocean of Profound Meaning', and the 'Dakini Heart Essence of Dzogchen' (Khandro Nyingthig [15]). It is based on many Dzogchen teachings from various terma (revealed treasure) traditions, and adorned with the personal instructions of the lama and my own experience.

---

13. **Padmasambhava** or "Guru Rinpoche" — 8th century Tantric Guru / Buddha.

14. The "**Seven Treasuries**" are a magnificent collection of writings by the 14th-century Nyingma master Longchen Rabjam: **The Wish-Fulfilling Treasury** (*Yishyin Dzö*); **Treasury of Pith Instructions** (*Mengak Dzö*); **Treasury of the Basic Space of Phenomena** (*Chöying Dzö*); **Treasury of Philosophical Tenets** (*Drubta Dzö*); **Treasury of the Supreme Vehicle** (*Tekchok Dzö*); **Treasury of Word and Meaning** *(Tsik Dön Dzö)*; and **The Treasury of the Natural State** (*Neluk Dzö*).

15. **Khandro Nyingthig** — The original transmission is attributed to Vimalamitra in the 8th century CE. Its key discoverer as a terma was Pema Ledrel Tsal in the 13th century, and it was significantly expanded and commented upon by Longchenpa in the 14th century.

Song 23 - Life is the Teaching

དད་ལྡན་གྱི་སློབ་མ་མང་པོ་ལ་ཕན་ཕྱིར་བཙུ་བདུད་རྩོགས་དྲུག་རང་གྲོལ་གྱིས་སྨྲས་པའོ། །

It was spoken by the renunciate Tsodruk Rangdrol [16] for the benefit of many faithful students.

འདིས་ཀྱང་བསྟན་པ་དང་སེམས་ཅན་ལ་ཕན་པ་དཔག་ཏུ་མེད་པ་འབྱུང་བའི་རྒྱུར་གྱུར་ཅིག །

May this also become a cause for immeasurable benefit to the teachings and sentient beings.

རྡོ་རྗེའི་གླུ་འདི་ནི་ཐར་པ་དོན་དུ་གཉེར་བའི་སྐལ་ལྡན་ཀུན་ལ་ཕན་ཕྱིར་བླངས་པ་ཡིན་པས། ལེན་པའི་དུས་ནི་རྣལ་འབྱོར་པས་ལྟ་བ་སྐྱོང་བའི་དུས་སུ་ཡིན་པའོ། །

Since this vajra song was sung for the benefit of all fortunate ones who seek liberation, the time to sing it is when a yogi is maintaining the view.

---

16. **Shabkar** (1781 to 1851 CE)

The Flight of Garuda

ལེན་ལུགས་ནི་རིག་འཛིན་ཤྲཱི་སིང་ཧའི་ཞལ་ནས། སངས་རྒྱས་ཀྱི་ཐུགས་ཁྱབ་གདལ་དུ་གནས། སེམས་ཅན་གྱི་རིག་པ་དུམ་བུར་གནས། ནམ་མཁའ་ལྟར་རྒྱ་བསྐྱེད་པ་དགོས་ཆེའོ། །

The way to sing it is according to the words of Vidyadhara Shri Singha [17]:

"The mind of the Buddha abides pervasively.
The awareness of sentient beings is scattered.
Expanding like the sky is most beneficial."

ཞེས་གསུངས་པ་ལྟར་རིག་པ་ནམ་མཁའ་ལྟར་རྒྱ་ཆེར་བསྐྱེད་དཔངས་བསྟོད་ཕུལ་ཡས་སུ་བཏད་ནས་སེམས་ཉིད་ཁྱབ་གདལ་ཡངས་པའི་ངང་ནས་རྡོ་རྗེའི་གླུ་འདི་འཐེན་དང་ལྟ་སྒོམ་དགོངས་འཕེལ་པའོ།། །།

As it is said, expand awareness greatly like the sky, raise its loftiness immeasurably, and then, with the mind in a state of pervasive vastness, sing this vajra song, and the view and meditation will improve.

---

17. **Shri Singha** (Sanskrit: Śrī Simha) – A core Dzogchen master from the 8th century CE. He was a principal disciple of Mañjuśrīmitra (the principal disciple of Garab Dorje) and is renowned for being the teacher of Padmasambhava, Vimalamitra, and Vairotsana, thus playing a crucial role in the early transmission of Dzogchen teachings to Tibet.

About Dr. Nida Chenagtsang

Born in Amdo, Malho, in Northeastern Tibet, Dr. Nida began his early studies of Sowa Rigpa at the local Tibetan medical hospital. Later, he was awarded a scholarship to enter the Lhasa Mentsikhang or Tibetan Medical University, where he completed his degree in 1996, with practical training at the Tibetan Medicine hospitals in Lhasa and Lhoka. Alongside his medical education, Dr. Nida trained in Vajrayana with teachers from every school of Tibetan Buddhism. In particular, he trained in the Longchen Nyingthig tradition of the Nyingma school with his root guru Ani Ngawang Gyaltsen and in the Dudjom Tersar tradition with Chönyi Rinpoche and Semo Dechen Yudrön. He received complete instruction in the Yuthok Nyingthig lineage, the unique spiritual tradition of Tibetan Medicine, from his teachers Khenpo Tsultrim Gyaltsen and Khenchen Troru Tsenam, and was requested to continue the Yuthok Nyingthig lineage by Jamyang Rinpoche of the Rebkong ngakpa and ngakma (i.e. non-monastic yogi and yogini) community.

A well-known poet in his youth, Dr. Nida later published many articles and books on Sowa Rigpa and the Yuthok Nyingthig tradition in Tibetan and English, which have been translated into several languages. He has extensively researched ancient Tibetan healing methods, and has gained acclaim in East and West for his revival of little-known Tibetan external therapies.

About Dr. Nida Chenagtsang

Dr. Nida is the Founder and Medical Director of the Sowa Rigpa Institute of Tibetan Medicine and the co-founder of the International Ngakmang Institute, which was established to preserve and support the unique Rebkong non-monastic yogi and yogini culture in modern Tibetan society. This is the first in a series of Sky Press publications dedicated to sharing this unique tradition of practice internationally. In addition to his work as a physician, Dr. Nida trains students in Sowa Rigpa and the Yuthok Nyingthig tradition in over forty countries around the world.

To learn about Dr Nida's publications please visit:
www.skypresspublications.com

www.ingramcontent.com/pod-product-compliance
Lightning Source LLC
Chambersburg PA
CBHW070134080526
44586CB00015B/1688